ALLOW Your
Vision to Soar!

A L LOW Your

to *Vision* *Soar*

This Message Just In! Trusting "the Voice" INside of You

Inspired by Kimberly West
Featuring 11 Visionaries!

AYSTS Publishing
Lighthouse Point, Florida

Allow Your Vision to Soar!

This Message Just IN–Trusting "the Voice" INside of YOU!

Co-Created with 11 Visionary's for
Transformation, Inspiration, Peace, Hope, Love & Joy!

©2012 Kimberly West

Contributing Authors

Kimberly West
Crystal Earley
Karen Binette Rapport & Leslie Bruce
Allison Turner
Susan Miller
Dr. Christine Chico
Carla Van Walsum
Laurina Anderson
Michelle Straka
Kathy Dedek
Becca Tebon

Published by:
AYSTS Publishing (a Division of Allow Your Spirit to Soar, Inc.)
15437 71st Drive North
Palm Beach Gardens, FL 33418

ISBN 978-0-9843061-1-4
Printed in the U.S.A.
Distributed by Allow Your Spirit to Soar Inc & Ingram Publishing

Editorial by: Kimberly West, Allison Turner & Deborah DeNicola
Type Design & Typography by: Juanita Dix
Cover Art & Design by: Juanita Dix
Photography by: Cynthia Lea Bautista Deery

CONTENTS

ACKNOWLEDGMENTS

Thank you Allison Turner, the VP of our company and partner in life! Also Dr. Christine Chico for believing in me and the Allow Your Spirit to Soar vision. I am humbled beyond words and am honored to have you on board this journey! I love you.

To the authors in this book: Crystal Earley, Leslie Bruce, Karen Binette Rapport, Allison Turner, Susan Miller, Dr. Christine Chico, Carla Van Walsum, Laurina Anderson, Michelle Straka, Kathy Dedek and Becca Tebon; thank you for sharing your story, knowledge and wisdom so others can learn they too can pursue their vision of owning a purpose driven business and that it's never too late to take your life back and soar! I love you.

To Suzanne Kovi, Jack Schulman, Judy Brown & Joe Hardesty: I will be eternally and forever grateful for your unconditional love, support and professionalism. Thank you for reminding me of my vision to help others soar and to get out of my own way! I love you all very much.

To the authors in our first book: Tim Kellis, Deborah DeNicola, Erin Currin, Jessica Garcia, Evelyn Ballin, Edward Rodriguez, Suzanne Kovi, Fran Asaro, Sara Doctofsky & Nancy Peña-Brink. I pray you are still sharing your story so others can soar. I love you very much!

To my mother, Beverly Ann Donahower; thank you for giving me birth and allowing me to be loved by someone else when you weren't able. What a selfless act you performed. I so enjoy sharing our story of forgiveness and how today we have come full circle. I love you.

To my brother, Kevin West; thank you for allowing me back in your life after years and years of chaos. I am so happy we are friends once more. You have no idea how you make my heart sing. I love you.

To my backend team that helped put this book together: Juanita Dix, our graphic designer, typesetter and formatter; Deborah DeNicola and Allison Turner, our editors; and Ingram Press, our distributor. Thank you! I love you.

To Nancy Matthews, Trish Carr and Susan Wiener founders of Women's Prosperity Network; I am so honored to be a part of your organization. Thank you for allowing me a space to Be Real, Get Real and Expect Real Results and never EVER judge me when that scared little girl showed up again. Your unconditional love has helped this Spirit Soar! I love you all.

To B. Brooke Peterson; thank you for being my "first" client in our Allow Your Vision to Soar program. You are a Spirit L.I.G.H.T. Coach and are soaring to new heights at 70 years young just by being who you were always meant to be. Keep teaching other's that it's never too late. I love you.

And last but certainly not least; Thank you God & the Amazing Universal Powers for ALLOWing me to experience in this lifetime what LIFE and owning a spiritual and purpose driven business is all about. I pray WE continue to serve you and others well. I love you all the most!

INTRODUCTION

Thank you for purchasing this second book in our Spiritual Enlightenment Series. My name is Kimberly West, the Founder of Allow Your Spirit to Soar, and the inspiration behind this vision.

As in my first book titled *Allow Your Spirit to Soar! No more Fear. No More Pain. No more Resentment. NO MORE!*, I believe not everyone is going to resonate with just one person's story or teachings. It is my intention to always co-create with heart centered, spiritual, positive human beings to give you a different perspective that will help you to ALLOW Your Spirit and Vision to Soar to places and heights you have never imagined you could go.

Inside this book you will learn from different women and their journeys who listened to the message they were given and then trusted "the Voice" inside of them to pursue a business from their passion & purpose.

At the writing of this book, I was asked this question several times. "Kimberly, as in your first book, why do you choose authors whom are not well known? Wouldn't you gain exposure more quickly or PR if you partnered with others who have made "their mark" on the world already?"

Without hesitation, my reply has been every single time. "They may not be well known; YET. I believe in my authors and what they do to make a difference in other's lives and their businesses. If I believe in them and their vision, give them a starting platform to tell their story and teach them about business and marketing along the way, then I have done my job. Its then up to them to take it from here and implement what they have learned. Many have named me Momma Butterfly. With my years of experience in business and the mission for Allow Your Spirit to Soar, our mission is to help them to spread their own wings so they can soar!"

So while you take the journey with us to learn how you too can trust "the Voice" INside of YOU, I pray you receive a plethora of tips, tools and techniques by reaching out to one of my authors or joining us in the Journey of Allow Your Spirit and Vision to Soar! Each author's contact information is provided at the beginning of their chapters. I pray you find "The One" (thank YOU Nancy Matthews!) that you may resonate with to help you along your path. This is YOUR life's journey my friends. May this book help you live it well and on purpose. God Bless!

KIMBERLY WEST is known as the "Soul See-er" & "Momma Butterfly" to her clients and many of her colleagues. She is also the creator of the *Allow Your Spirit to Soar* brand. She is passionate about co-creating a space that allows people to be who they truly are so they can trust their vision and live their purpose.

With over three decades of marketing and advertising experience, including successfully owning and operating her own company's, Kimberly knows that any business must have both a bold vision and an action plan to succeed. Although her past company's focused on strategic marketing plans for her clients, she found she had a talent for pulling visions out of people, and then helped them give birth to their dreams in a very real way.

Her ability and dedication to this was fueled by her own traumatic past, which required her to overcome profound obstacles in

1

order to live the life and create the business she wanted. Through her marketing consulting, she became committed to sharing the message that anyone can live the life they were meant to live, regardless of what happened in the past.

Kimberly incorporated this spirit into her advertising and marketing business, helping her clients in a very unique way.

She then experienced a catalyst moment that caused her own bold "shift" in late 2011. Although she enjoyed helping her clients become successful at KB Business Consultants, Inc. with her marketing knowledge and expertise; she realized her strongest and highest calling was in being a spiritual mentor first, that would allow people to trust their inner voice and move towards their purpose, regardless of past occurrences or current circumstances.

Kimberly took a bold leap of faith and decided to put all her time and efforts into her brand, Allow Your Spirit to Soar. She quickly gained clientele and now works with people from all over the world, helping them to discover their deepest desire and purpose. She is committed to supporting her clients so they have the courage to follow their vision, as well as providing them with spiritual support and practical marketing techniques to ensure their vision comes to completion. She believes it is never too late to find and follow your dream and that no vision is too small.

DEDICATION

I dedicate my chapter to you, the one who is reading this book. May God Bless you and yours, today and always.

Chapter One

This Message Just IN!
by Kimberly West

With reading my chapter, I want you to know and FEEL you can do and be whatever you want to be in your life and business no matter what has happened in your past. Both of my company's were recently evaluated at 250k by a professional CPA firm. I share this with you not to impress you. I share this with you because IF I would have allowed my past human labels control who I am today, I wouldn't be living the life of my dreams. Allow me share a bit of my past. It was ruled by violence, drugs and fear, until I started my journey of awakening in 2006. IF I would have listened to "society" and what "others" say you need to be a success in the world, I would not be living in a 4700 square foot home which we have turned into a space for others to learn how to ALLOW their Spirits and Visions to Soar! It all started when I learned to TRUST "the Voice" INside of Me, which I choose to call God and the Amazing

Universal Powers. Every time I do, they never EVER let me down. If you want to learn more about my past human labels, please buy our first book. Enough of the darkness, now on to the light!

So I ask. Do you know how to trust "the Voice" INside of You? Do you listen to the messages you are given every single day to live a life of joy? Do you passionately love what you do to make a living? After being involved with "Corporate America" for years full of competition and greed, I can finally say . . . YES!!! I LOVE what I do because I am the leader of the business of MY dreams created from my passion to help others soar!

I would like to share with you my *"Vision Statement"* for our company.

Allow Your Spirit Soar, Inc. is a business helping others learn first and foremost, to listen to the "the Voice" inside of them. We help others release who they truly are, by starting with their Spirit. For those who want to start their own business, from that space, we co-create heart centered, inspirational, purpose driven businesses. We provide continual support with the education they are in search of through creating "Spirit & Vision Shops", 1& 2 day retreats at our "By Invitation Only" center, offering one-on-one mentoring packages, creating VISION-Mentoring groups including an on-line membership that offers a plethora of educational tele-seminar and webinars to stay surrounded with like-minded human beings to consistently remind others of their greatness!

Do you have a vision statement for your business? How about your life? I highly encourage creating one of your own and read it every morning before you start your day. This does one of two things. It not only reminds you of your passion but puts a vibration out to the Universe of what people, places and things you need to show up to allow your vision to come to fruition much quicker. I am still in awe to this day of how simple and true this is. Allow me to share one of the miracles that showed up in my journey.

Since being awakened, it doesn't matter what time I go to bed. I wake up between 5 and 5:30am and head outside to meditate and listen to the messages. After the launch of our first book on 1-22-11, I was sitting outside in nature, thanking God and the Amazing Universal Powers for what had just occurred. This was our 2nd Conference as well and was a great success. However, I asked God, now what? I heard "the Voice" say very loud and clear. Take a group of 9 on a Spiritual Retreat to Sedona on 11-11-11. You will find even more answers you are search of and those who attend will find more of their answers to their life's journey too.

I said, out loud in the darkness of the morning, Sedona? What in the world is in Sedona? I have never ever been to Sedona. Why Sedona? And "the Voice" said very clearly; "We have co-created the World Wide Web for a reason. Go use it." Yes they have a sense of humor too!

The very first website I clicked was about the Spiritual Vortexes and the Energy of Sedona! Since I teach clients about how to use energy to create their amazing life, I simply smiled for I knew without a doubt what I was supposed to do. I have never EVER put together a retreat before or traveled to Sedona for goodness sakes, now what do I do? Then POOF like magic, Bunny Muter, who is one of the most amazing travel agents in the world, showed up. She assisted me to make this happen. We launched the vision I received from "the Voice" and the retreat sold out at $1500 per person plus airfare in a matter of 4 months. Yes, lives were changed and true authentic friendships were made that will last a lifetime by listening to "the Voice" inside of me. I was also told I would find the love of my life. Yes, that happened too.

I make it a daily practice to listen to "the Voice", well most of the time for I am still human. If I didn't, I wouldn't be writing this chapter, been able to attract my perfect partner who is the VP of our company blessed with two investors.

So I ask you once more? Do you listen; really listen to "the Voice" INside of YOU? OR do you listen to all of the mental noise going on in the world? How about the naysayers who want to steal your dream? Are you truly following your spirit and vision of what you want in this lifetime? If not, what is holding you back from breaking FREE from those chains? The only answer is you.

On the Allow Your Spirit to Soar Facebook page is where I first started sharing my messages I received. I would like to share just some of them with you now and how this vision for this book came about.

This Message Just IN! Say N.O. Come on you can do it. N.O. nnnnnnnooooooo :)

This Message Just IN! IF you don't like where YOUR Life's Journey is headed then change your thoughts which will change your energy which will change your path! Start with a Thank YOU God and the Amazing Universal Powers when you first get UP then finish it with...Let's Rock! Now get UP there and CREATE a Magnificent Day! WE love YOU!

This Message Just IN! Never EVER Allow a "Red Flag" to continue to fly when IT shows up in the beginning of any relationship be it personal or business! You can throw love and light on "it" but don't try to save or fix the flag. Look for a Green one instead!

This Message Just IN! Set you intentions to ONLY have a good day. YOU are the creator of YOUR experiences. Every single human being that crosses YOUR Life Journey is because of what YOU want

YOUR Life to be. Think Peace, Love, Joy, Happiness, Compassion, Forgiveness in 24 hours and experience the sweetness of Life!

This Message Just IN! Get off the computer, go tell someone your love them A LOT and give them a BIG OLE HUG!!!

This Message Just IN! There is no such thing as HELL! There is no such thing as a FEARFUL GOD! There is no such thing as EVIL! UNLESS that is what YOU believe. If you are going to AL-LOW these restrictions into YOUR Life's Journey, why not think of happy things...like HEAVEN, a LOVING & UNCONDITIONAL GOD & JOY! Then watch your frown turn INto a Smile!!! Our Minds are Powerful my friends...use IT peacefully!

This Message Just IN! When you over-commit you are not serving anyone's higher being well...especially YOU!

This Message Just IN! Live YOUR Life IN Light, Love and a Whole Lot of Laughter!!! YOU ONLY have one chance this time. Whatcha gonna do now? Uh...whatcha gonna do NOW! ALLOW Your Spirit to Soar!!!

This Message Just IN! It's OK to not know the answer. AL-LOW the Mystery to UNFOLD, all in due time. ALLOW-Shift™! ALLOW-Shift™! ALLOW-Shift™! May YOU be blessed today BE-YOND Your Wildest Imagination!!! Your thoughts! Your Life's Journey! Dream HUGE!

This Message Just IN! Be true to YOUR Body, Mind & Spirit! You only get ONE chance in this lifetime. ALLOW Your Spirit to Soar!!!

This Message Just IN! For those humans out there who continue to do the same things over and over and over and over again expecting different results, did you know "they" consider that insanity? OR it could be that YOU refuse to give up until you reach the desired outcome. You see it's all in YOUR perception now isn't it? As long as YOU are Happy with what YOU are doing, that's OK! This is YOUR Life's Journey!

This Message Just IN! When your body, mind and spirit say stop...stop! Turn off all electronics and Just Be!

This Message Just IN! What will YOU do today that will leave an impression in someone's life? How will YOU show UP? What one little, bitsy, itsy, tiny thing can YOU do that will make someone's day? Run a small errand? Write a hand written note? Take someone for a walk in nature or Just Be with someone who is lonely? ALLOW their Spirit to Soar by one random act. YOU will be glad you did!

Now here's the reality and my truth. Even though I have been living this way for the last seven years, I honestly listen to "the Voice" only 97% of the time. With the growth of this company, I ALLOWed myself to be taken away from the peaceful, loving, joyful human BEing I AM, by ALLOWing "others" and the lower levels of energy to take me away from my amazing life and the mission of Allow Your Spirit to Soar on many occasions. Yes I am still human, and that's OK!

Here's the great news! Thank GOD you can start from right here, right now to listen to "the Voice" INside of you once more. I know the secret to living a blessed life but it takes daily practice to stay there. I simply step back into this amazing way to live, let go of any person, place or thing that doesn't serve my higher being and get out of my way once more.

Here's another reason why I am passionate about my vision. You finish a program or just leave a conference all pumped up ready to soar, then BAM you allow the negative people, places and things to bring you back down into the little you once more. Can you relate to this? I see this happening all of the time and I am guilty of ALLOWing this to happen to me as well. This is why I co-created a space both virtually and live to help you stay in the light in this challenging world we have all created today.

You see, my friends, it's never EVER too late to trust "the Voice" INside of YOU. It's learning how to listen, really listen. With much practice, you too will get to the point when you are given the message, you won't think about the how; you will just go! However, sometimes we have to be reminded by someone else if we are on the right path. Allow me to share another example.

While in Sedona, I was told by not one, not two but three physics that I am a great leader of a spiritually based business. Even knowing what I know, I still needed confirmation that I was on the right path. Silly human. All of them saw me as a great Chief in my past life. I was seeing "tribes" in the Red Rocks all week with me as the Chief! Now this is where it gets a tad freaky and where my life's journey has finally come full circle.

Once I found my biological family, I found out I was of Cherokee dissent. I had an imaginary friend called Chi Chi Waa. Being raised in a strict Catholic environment, I was told I was WRONG and there was no such thing. However, as a 6-year old I adamantly said, yes there is. She is right here. Don't you see her?

Then I wanted a horse so bad. No one in my adoptive family ever owned horses. I kept seeing the horse and what she looked like. First was Peggy Sue, a Shetland pony which I broke my self. Then finally my dream horse showed up! I would take off like the wind bare back on my thoroughbred which I named, Mystic Blush. She was my favorite and she became my best friend. She understood me. I wanted to be with her 24/7. I had no fear of any animal. They were all my friends. I loved being out with nature and talking with the trees. Looking back now I see my journey into my spirituality started at 6-years old. However, organized religion and the uneducated metaphysical and spiritually deprived minds of my parents stopped me from being who I truly was from the very beginning. In return, I felt caged and created all kinds of "not-so-good" experiences, which led me to a path of destruction for a very long time. All I wanted to do was soar and be me!

As time went on, I did what "society" wanted me to do and what I thought would make everyone else happy. I wanted to be a millionaire. I wanted that American Dream! Yeah, that would fix everything! NOT.

I built the successful company, lived in a big house, drove the nice car, wore the nicest suits, (pant suits of course) and ate at the finest restaurants. I was on TOP of my game, until I got another 2x4 over my head, and I lost it all. What am I doing so wrong? Why is all of this happening to me? Then I realized it wasn't happening to me, it was happening for me.

I will now share with you how Allow Your Spirit to Soar was born and finally found my way back home.

I moved to Florida in 2005 and started KB Business Consultants, Inc. I made 20K my first month in business. After watching the movie "The Secret" in 2006, and being in a very unhealthy marriage, I started being awakened once more to my true Spirit. I started digging deep, I mean really deep into the Spiritual and Metaphysical way of being once more. I would go outside and the trees formed the shapes of great Native American Chiefs. I started talking with the trees once more. That was the day "the Voice" came back and I listened. I finally listened and trusted the message they had been trying to give me since I was a child. This time I got to make my own choices because I was a 45-year old adult! But wait! What would "society" say? That I am crazy? That I am light years ahead of what the world would be able to accept as normal? I don't care what others say! I AM TRUSTING "the Voice" INside of ME for once in my life!

So while on this journey, I had somewhat incorporated the spiritual aspect into my business, to only go back to what I felt I would not be judged on. I was miserable once more. Until one day, yep sitting out in nature, I asked God and the Amazing Universal Powers a question that would forever change my journey for good.

I asked. "Ok God, I have the successful business again, I am helping others learn how to market and grow their business, I am using my Kreative Braynz, but I am still not happy. Really, really happy! Then out of nowhere came the most beautiful blue butterfly and "the Voice" INside of me speaking to me in an Angelic voice. "My child, you are not ALLOWing Your Spirit to Soar!" OMG! How many 2x4's does it take for goodness sakes? In my case it was Sequoia's!

I immediately went inside; waited until my CPA woke up and said let's get this vision started NOW! I don't care what the others say. We are going to teach others how to Allow their Spirits to Soar!

The rest is herstory as they say. Here we are 2.5 years later, launching our 2nd book and gearing up for our 3rd Annual Conference called VISION QUEST 2012!

So you see my friends. You truly can be and do whatever you want to be IF you learn how to ALLOW Your own Spirit and Vision to Soar. But here's one key to true success! Surround yourself with like-minded human beings who you can co-create with to take your vision to the next level. By collaborating with the "collective consciousness" your Spirit will have no choice but to soar!

To live a spiritual life every day, it takes consistent practice of staying IN the light!

Allow me to give you a few simple steps to begin your journey into another dimension of how to live a life of pure joy.

1) Find a day where you can read each one of my author's chapters in one sitting. Then reach out to them and ask for their help. You will find their information at the end of each of their chapters.

2) Get up 15 minutes early each morning to meditate, journal, exercise or work on your marketing & business plan for your vision, BEFORE you take care of anyone else. At the writing of this chapter, I have not been doing this enough myself. This is where "the Voice" INside of YOU will start to show UP and support you on your mission.

3) Turn off the news. They want to keep you sick and stuck! The banks, the government, the doctors, the politicians, the marketers, and the media want you to live in fear, save your house by paying higher property taxes or a higher interest rate, vote for another president that later you will blame for the demise of our country, or buy something bigger and better that is going to fix the outside of you. Remember, what you ALLOW into your energy and mind is the reality you will create!

4) Write out your one-week personal, business (if you have one), strategic and tactical goals on Monday morning. Create a realistic plan and don't over commit! Start with one a day. Then add more once you reach one a day. One is better than

none!

5) Don't lie, steal, cheat or blame anyone else for your demise. Take your power back and be responsible for your choices.

6) Don't take yourself so seriously. Laugh until it hurts. Allow your inner child to come back out and play!

7) Don't allow yourself to be compared to others. You are perfect just the way you are. Surround yourself with only those who support you and who you can fully support back. Quit trying to fit a square peg into a round hole!

8) When you are stressed, don't post your anger on Facebook or any other social media platform. This causes a horrible ripple effect and people will use your moment of weakness against you. Walk away until you can come from a place of peace, hope, love & joy! This is how God wants us to be.

9) Know that nothing in your past life has happened to you; it has happened for you. If you want to know about my past experiences, both in life and in business, please buy our first book or the ALLOW-Shift™ System. I learned that the energy you put on something that wasn't so good in your past, you will re-create the same experiences over and over and over. My past experiences is not my reality today. YOU create your own reality from right here, right now!

10) Don't judge anyone. You have no right. It's their journey. Live only yours.

11) Find a mentor with whom you resonate. This is

YOUR spirit & vision. Ask for references before hiring another with this very important role. I invite you to "play in our world" or one of my authors that will help your body, mind, spirit and vision to soar.

There are many other tips and tools I can share; however, I want you to read my authors' chapters and learn from them as well. You see, my friends, this vision has never EVER been about me, it's always been about the "collective consciousness" which is why the name of my company or brand is NOT Kimberly West. It is and always will be Allow Your Spirit to Soar. I am simply the lead messenger and the Chief Enlightenment Officer (CEO)of our tribe. I pray WE serve you well!

The Spirit IN Me, Honors the Spirit IN YOU!
Kimberly West aka Momma Butterfly
Kimberly is the inspiration behind her collaborative books, an author, has been a featured speaker at many conferences. She has appeared on both television and radio. Additionally, she is co-creating a myriad of "Spirit & Vision" workshops, info products and a membership website. For more information contact the Allow Your Spirit to Soar office at (561) 529-2369 or visit our website to receive your FREE Positive and Wealth Affirmations at www.AllowYourSpiritToSoar.com

CRYSTAL EARLEY is a Certified Health Coach and is committed to helping people suffering from obesity choose the path of love and self-respect, and to change their lives by experiencing healthy living.

Crystal's turning point came when she temporarily lost her eyesight due to a diabetic spike; she had to make a decision whether or not she wanted to live. She chose life, lost over three hundred pounds and is still losing. The transformation, in her health and life, made Crystal realize she was passionate about helping others get healthy bodies, healthy lives and love themselves by getting healthy one step at a time.

Knowing there is always a bigger story behind why people become overweight, Crystal is passionate about helping clients to understand their past so they can triumph from the darkness of their past, to the light of the present and future. Her sensible and compassionate approach to healthy eating and exercise, combined with her motivational style of delivery and personal understanding of obesity, has helped hundreds of people change their lives and embrace health.

Crystal never gives up on people. Her clients say she is inspiring, a generous nurturer and supporter, and has an innate ability to understand what they want and need. Her belief and message of, "One meal at a time; one pound at a time," has been the catalyst for her clients to have the courage to change.

Crystal is a professional speaker and has been featured on various radio talk shows and webinars. To learn more, please visit website at www.gethealthywith.tsfl.com or contact her at crystalearley@comcast.net.

DEDICATION

I dedicate this chapter to my loving husband extraordinaire and best friend whose strength and support has helped me believe in me and achieve so much that most would think unattainable. Your love and guidance brings inspiration. Also to my loving parents, sister and her husband who are an amazing family that always supported me in every endeavor no matter how crazy. Friends and clients thank you for your continued friendships and support. I love you all.

Chapter Two

Transformation of Mind, Body and Soul!
by Crystal Earley

Let's start with my body. I have been heavy all my life except at birth when I was a normal 6 lbs 4 oz. Then my weight just climbed. My mom said I would eat anything and loved blueberry buckle. I was the chubby kid being made fun of. Name calling, at that age, leaves an impression on your soul. Bullying is an epidemic that has been going on for way too long and needs to be stopped! I was chased, teased, and tortured by classmates. In third grade the school nurse decided I needed to be on a diet so I was made to weigh in every Friday. The entire class laughed at me when I was told to go weigh in. I think back and wonder why my parents allowed this to happen. Should it not have been them to make this decision and help me through this difficult time?

That year at Christmas, our class had a gift exchange where you brought a gift to put under the tree, putting girl or boy on the tag. I brought a blue jewelry box to give. When I received a chocolate Santa, the teacher declared in front of the entire class that I could not have it. She asked for a volunteer to trade and one of my classmates jumped up and said she would because she got a stupid jewelry box. I was embarrassed and crushed.

Gym class was always a nightmare. The Presidential test where you climbed the rope was horrifying. Once again I was ridiculed by both teacher and students. Then there was recess. I could go on and on about the bullying I experienced from being overweight but the bottom line is - I hated school!

Because my father was in the Air Force, we moved, when I was nine, to Germany. The food in Germany has a high caloric value. The first night we were there we went to a small restaurant where the waiter said everyone gets their own pizza. Are you kidding me? Each of us had a small pizza. Well, we traveled a lot and ate a lot. Germany has divine pastries. I did like school there and had many friends; they seemed to be more accepting of me. Then we moved back to the states, and I turned thirteen a week later.

The teen years were really rough. We lived with my Grandma while my parents looked for a house. I loved her but she was funny and confusing; in one breath she told me I was chunky and in the next breath offered me a cookie. She baked a lot and always gave us cookies while we did homework. As soon as dinner dishes were cleared we were offered dessert every night and on weekends, after lunch, it was fruit and vanilla ice cream. By high school I was in the two hundreds, really unhappy and depressed. I had a lot of friends, did well in school but felt empty inside. During the summer band camp before senior year, a fellow band member was relentless about my weight, saying things like my parents must spend a fortune on my clothes because of the yardage. So my senior year I decided to do something about my weight; this time it was my decision, not that of a doctor, teacher, nurse or my parents like in the past. I never remember not being on a DIET or cutting portions except at Grandma's; she was a feeder. But this time I decide I would graduate and be 'normal' like my friends. I asked my Mom about a program I saw in the paper so she went with me and we did it together. We both did great!

I was almost to goal with about 25 lbs to go and prom came along. I was house sitting for my boss from the vacuum telemarketing firm where I worked, and a friend was staying with me. A vacuum salesman, who was a friend (or so I thought), stopped over to take us to dinner since we were not going to prom. His wife had just had a baby and was in the hospital, so I thought that was really nice of him to think of us. After dinner my girl friend got a call to go home so I told the guy I needed to iron clothes for tomorrow, but he wanted to hang out to talk. I never felt uncomfortable or threatened; after all, he was a friend. He followed me upstairs where I started ironing then all of a sudden he pushed me on the bed. Next thing I knew he was on top of me - so violent! I was still a virgin who never had even experimented other than to kiss a boy. When he left I showered with scalding hot water trying to scrub the shame and dirtiness off of me; I felt such shame. Had I somehow asked for this? Had I led him on or acted interested? What did I do? I must have done something. He was married and had a new child. After the shower, I stripped the bed, took it downstairs and scrubbed with all my might to get the blood stains out, thinking I can't let anyone find out. What would people think of me?

The next morning I picked up my younger sister and we went to work at the Polo field where we were usherettes which I had always loved. I had been usherette of the year for two years in a row. My sister, friends and boss asked me if something was wrong, but I said I was just tired and up too late.

After that night I did not care about friends, school work or anything and went into a depression where I almost did not graduate because I simply did not care. When I returned to school, I learned a close male friend had been killed that same night which affected me too. He always joked with me; having three classes together made the day go by quicker but now he was gone. Then on top of everything I was dealing with, my period did not come. Could I be pregnant? I had always dreamed of being a mom, married and happy. What was I to do? I still had told no one except my boss and did not plan on it. How could I tell my parents who raised us to find love, get married, and then have children? Turns out I wasn't pregnant, just stressed. I contemplated suicide for a brief moment. I had let the rape affect my life so terribly that it was out of control, not trusting or caring about anyone or anything. What do I do? I graduated by the grace of God and a teacher who I know must have gone to bat for me.

After graduation, I really did not know what direction to take my life so I went to nail school. I was in and out of bad relationships and gaining weight because after all the weight had protected me; it was my shelter. I dated a real bad boy my parents did not like. I was having sex because I didn't have anything special to hold onto for a husband since it had been taken away. Right? Well, I became pregnant, did not tell my mom but confided in my younger sister, who was only 14. She had a nightmare, that I was being hurt by the baby's father so she told my mom. When my mom, with hurt in her eyes, confronted me, asking how I could have sex out of wedlock after how they raised me, I said I had nothing to protect because it had been taken from me. So my poor mother had two terrible shocks in one night.

My father was away on business. She told him about the baby but not the rape. She took me to a counselor but that did not help except make me realize it was not my fault. My father was so hurt and disappointed that he could not speak to me. If I answered the phone and there was silence I knew it was him, so I would get my mom. The silence was unbearable. I was always so close to him but now he was a thousand miles away physically and emotionally. If I had told him about the rape it might have made a difference, but I will never know. When he found out ten years later, his anger for what I had gone through showed his love and understanding.

I was three months pregnant when they found out. The boy's parents were called and plans were made to set us up in an apartment. I thought my life was coming together. Eventually dad would forgive me, right? Well, the next month my boyfriend's friend was drinking and I wanted to go home. I knew we should not stay there. His friend, a real loser, got furious and kicked me hard in the stomach saying I should know my place. While I should have gone to the hospital, I did not until the next afternoon when the pain was so bad and I started bleeding. My mom met us there. I was losing the baby, and they had to do a DNC. It was so painful and the doctor on call was an uncompassionate human being. During the procedure when I said the pain was too much to bear, he said, "You thought you could go through child birth, what a joke." After childbirth there is a reward, but after this I had nothing. He was unbelievable!!

I know everything happens for a reason, but this experience was hard. I stayed in bed for three weeks. My Dad finally spoke to me and told me he was sorry for his reaction to the pregnancy and that I had lost the baby. My parents were very supportive of me but still had their suspicions of my boyfriend. I continued seeing the guy, but not long after I realized he was everything my parents said he was and more. He was a thief, cheat and liar, so I left him. More losers came, too many. I tried to always be the supportive, loving girlfriend. I met someone I thought truly cared for me and we got engaged. While I thought I was happy, my parents were not happy; he was ten years older than me. Not long after our engagement, I realized he started treating me like a piece of property. Six months into our engagement, he cheated on me with my girl friend, so I lost two people in my life.

I dove into my career, working at different restaurants, building my reputation for doing public relations. Soon I was a manager of a small cafe at 19-years old, steadily increasing my portfolio. By the age of 21, I was running five restaurants. Running that many at once was physically and mentally challenging but I realized I had to make time for me and somehow I found time to start dating again. Meanwhile the restaurant owners, who were minorities and had contracts with the local government, decided they were not renewing the contracts and I was out of a job.

What do I do now? I was burned out with the long hours I had been working so I thought what do I really want to do? I decided I wanted to work with children because I still felt the loss of my baby. I ached to just feel that unconditional love that a child gives. I baby sat a ton when younger and even worked for a nanny agency during summers. So I looked in the paper, found a few jobs but nothing felt right until I met Savannah's family. She was only five-weeks old. I fell in love with her and her family. We bonded quickly. I felt guilty in a way because I was there for so many of her firsts. To this day she calls me Nanny and our families are connected with a special bond. I treated her as if she were my own. She means so much to me and healed my soul. Watching her grow up and being a part of her life is so amazing and means so much to my family.

When dating again, I met another loser, an alcoholic. Of course, I did not realize it at first. He was so dreamy, why would he want me?

Settle for me? It was not long before I realized he was not perfect but he never harassed me about my weight; that lasted six months when he told me he would marry me if I lost weight. Was he serious? He was not perfect, was he going to change? If you love someone do you make them change? Was I wrong? So it became a destructive relationship; I started drinking with him and not eating. One night it is like God himself said wake up! You want this life and another addiction? He had just totaled my car on my birthday after he disappeared, supposedly to get my birthday gift. The next day I got the call; thank God no one was hurt in the accident, but I decided I was definitely through. So I said goodbye to him.

At twenty-four years old I had been in many different bad relationships, but I finally met a good guy whom I married. I was about a size 22 but I decided I wanted a size 10-12 wedding gown. This time, I was going to make it happen. I was happy, had a man who loved me, the real me, my soul. So I went to a doctor and was put on a diet and told to take fen-phen. Having returned to restaurant management, I fell on a shift, badly hurt my ankle, and had to take steroids. Talk about depressing! I had become a size 18, so close, yet it seemed miles away from my goal. Without being able to walk much and taking steroids, I gained weight quickly. Becoming more depressed, I stopped eating everything except dinner so I gained weight quickly. As I laid there watching my body betray my dream, growing every day, every dress fitting was a nightmare; I was bigger and bigger by the day so when I got married I was a size 28W. How did this happen? My fiancée still adored me, and I wondered how he could possibly love the person I had become?

We had a beautiful wedding and I became comfortable in my body. We ate out a lot, enjoyed life and I put on more weight. We were trying to have children, but I was diagnosed with a thyroid problem which shocked me because a doctor I saw fifteen years earlier said it was fine. Now I found out my thyroid was dead, I needed medication and pregnancy was not looking possible! All I ever wanted was to be a mom and now I had the perfect husband, a man I knew would be a great father. I internalized everything and fed the emptiness. When I was young, I went shopping with mom and we got a treat, but we always had to get rid of the evidence. If dad did not know, it did not count. When I shopped as an adult, I never ate a whole cake or pizza but would get M&Ms or something. I was not eating breakfast and really did not start eating till 4:00 but then ate what I wanted. I got heavier and heavier and it was getting harder to move around so my hubby waited on me. When I went to stores I used an electric scooter. I could not fit in theater seats, booths or chairs with arms at restaurants. I had to buy two airline seats so I was not encroaching on someone's space. Having to ask for a seatbelt extension was so embarrassing because they announce it, "seat C22 needs an extension." Have some compassion! The airplane bathrooms are too small. I could never eat or drink when flying because I could not fit in the small enclosure. Sometimes the pain of needing to go became unbearable.

Life was rolling out of control; I was slowly drowning in my weight and more health problems. As the weight climbed, I became ill more often. I was diagnosed with diabetes and asthma and had terrible attacks. Sometimes my lungs would just start to close. I was once hospitalized for ten days, put on prednisone and again watched my body swell; it took almost five months to get weaned off of it since you have to lower the doses slowly. I thought okay it's time to do something, so I started trying to get healthy. I started eating salads almost every time we went out and almost always heard someone talking about me. "Does she know how big she is?" or "It looks like she has eaten enough for a life time."

It was so hard to go out with friends or family. I always got there early so I could get a table with chairs with no arms. If I got to the restaurant and they were sitting where I could not fit, I wanted to die when I had to ask the waitress to move us. Hostesses could be so rude about it. One time a hostess carried a chair for me over her head through the restaurant seating us in the center; I felt like the entertainment for the evening - the fat lady has come to eat for all to see. One night we went out to celebrate my sister's birthday. I freaked out because the restaurant only had seating outside to accommodate my size. With the wait, my brother-in-law said we would take the booth available. I thought I won't fit but how can I leave? It's her birthday so I can't leave. It was a special night, so I endured the humiliation of sitting in a chair at the end of the table. Several times I had to get up so people could get by and was then hit in the head by waiters' trays.

I decided I had too much and went to therapy to help with my feelings; I saw an ad in the paper that said hypnosis could help with weight loss. She helped me discover and uncover a lot of emotions. One time she had me under and told me to think of my first bad memory when I felt hurt or upset. I was only two-years old; my sister had just been born and was getting a lot of attention. Mom had her lying on the couch and was in the kitchen while grandma and grandpa were in the living room with us. I walked over picked up my new born sister like a football, holding her under my arm by the neck. My grandfather started screaming, "put her down are you trying to kill her?" and my mom ran into the room, took my sister from me and my grandma took me to the kitchen to try to calm me down reassuring me my sister was fine. She gave me a few cookies and I was fine. Grandpa did not speak to me for the rest of his two-week visit. I heard the story before because our family jokes that this is why my sister has such a beautiful long neck that no one else in the family has. So I asked Mom if this was the real story, and she agreed. So the therapist said I associated or felt love when given the cookies which explains wanting sweets when things go bad.

Next we uncovered what the rapist said which I had blocked out of my mind. The last thing he said before he left was, "Just think when you lose the rest of your weight." So I related getting thin to violence and bodily harm. As an adult I realize I should have pressed charges but as a teenager all I thought about was his poor wife being in the hospital with that new little baby. I now realize I did ruin it by not letting her know what and who she was married to; she deserved to know. I shared it with our boss and he lost his job, so at least I never had to see him again. It was a violent way to lose my virginity. So something I had been brought to believe you don't do until marriage was not so important. What was the big deal?

Being married, I now know it is a beautiful, intimate passion that two people share. I learned a lot, grew as a person, and the therapist helped me change a lot of habits. I was becoming more involved in the church, was happy, but my weight was still high. Actually, I did not even know how high. I was hospitalized for severe asthma and again given steroids. I had diabetes, asthma and continued getting sicker. When I saw a doctor he would say lose weight so you won't get so sick and I replied very angrily, "Thin people get sick, thin people have diabetes and thin people have asthma!" I was so angry!!

Then I went to purchase a new car and I did not fit behind the wheel. The salesman, who we always bought our cars from, said we will take the seat out, extend the track, and you will be fine but I knew no one could sit behind me and I did not want the car built around me. I bought a car that fit me better but was still dangerous because the wheel could get stuck in my stomach.

COMING FROM THE DARKNESS TO THE LIGHT

Then I had my God moment. God woke me from the dark! I say he hit me over the head with a Sequoia tree taking my sight so I may see the light. My husband and I went to the drive-in movies, and I had eaten well that day with no sugar, but I was so thirsty; I could not quench my thirst with bottle after bottle of water, many trips to restroom, and missing 3/4 of the movie. The movie ended and my hubby drove home. When we pulled on to the road I told him that all the street signs were blurry; I was usually known as hawk eyes.

Hubby said, "You are tired, close your eyes, and I will wake you when we get home." Twenty minutes later he shook my shoulder gently saying, "We are home honey."

I woke with a start because I could not see!!

He said, "Stop joking around."

"I can't see; I hear you but can't see you!"

Talk about terrifying! We contacted my doctor who said my sugar must have spiked. While my hubby tried to check it, the machine kept saying error which meant my sugar was over 500. Yikes! So over the next few days I was given more and more medicine to get it down. The first two days were very scary and a big wake-up call. For three weeks my vision was just a little blurry.

So the doctor said I needed gastric bypass so almost instantly the diabetes would be under control. I didn't want that because I knew people who died from it. Now the hard pill to swallow was I never knew how much I weighed. At most I thought I weighed 350-375. Scales go to 350 at most doctor offices which I always refused to get on, but now he insisted. It would not weigh me. I was so upset and we now had to find a place to weigh me and the number was 545. I was devastated to say the least! I cried and cried, and my mom and husband could not believe it. We were all in denial! I also think that when people really love you they don't see weight. So the doctor said to me, "You think you will die during surgery but you are going to die now because you weigh almost 600 lbs." I wanted to die but I loved my husband and wanted a future with him, so I prayed. "Please God, help me, point me the right direction, save me, you created me and I have ruined and abused your creation. I am sorry! Please save me and don't let me die, I have a lot of life to live."

God answered my prayers when I was reintroduced to someone I had not seen in six months and she had lost 50 pounds. When she explained how, I continued to believe it was one more thing to fail at. Like most, I thought where is the magic pill? So I told her I would think about it but I was thinking that surgery was my only hope even though it scared me to death. She encouraged me to try this first because surgery is so drastic and final. God bless her persistence because she called me four times over the next ten days until I agreed. I told hubby I have nothing to lose but weight. If you do the surgery, they want you to do a pre-surgery diet to show your dedication. After starting, I felt great by the fifth day and told my hubby, "I believe I can do this."

Within five months of being on the program, my sugar was normal with no more medications, shots or asthma medications. Remember my sister's birthday which was September 9th? February 25th was my parent's anniversary and my dad wanted to go back to that restaurant; I, of course, freaked but went. When taken to a booth, I said a prayer, "Please God, I have worked so hard, come so far, please use a shoe horn if necessary but squeeze me into this booth!" I not only fit but had room in front of me! I cried out, "I fit, I really fit! Thank God!" My sweet sister (always a small framed 110 lbs), who never seem to notice her big sister was huge, said, "Yeah so?" She didn't remember her birthday and had no idea I was that uncomfortable. I started to cry and she took a picture of me pointing to the space between me and the table. We celebrated our parent's anniversary and my weight loss.

As of the writing of this book, I have lost 300 lbs in 34 months. I love eating healthy and my life is wonderful. Hubby joined me and lost 150 lbs. Life is so different; we do things that we were unable to do before. I now fit in booths, chairs, and one airplane seat with no seatbelt extension. I became a health coach and help others reclaim their health and life. I am so passionate about it that it does not even feel like work. I am determined to help others love themselves. I know what obstacles they have and have compassion to help them through the journey. My soul is healing and those marks left by bullies are fading. I want the bullies of the world to know the damage they can cause. I believe parents need to take a stronger hold on what they teach their children in treatment of others. I sometimes wonder what is going through a parent's mind when they hear their child being rude or hateful. Do they really see that as acceptable behavior? I'm sure they have not been taught any better, so we are dealing with generations of rude, ill-behaved individuals. I pray for them.

I know God is helping my healing. My spiritual faith has become stronger over the last few years. I have attended the same church for twenty-one years, always attending but sitting in the back row. I am more involved now, assisting the Pastor once a month, participating in the women's group and going on retreats. Having faith can get you through anything. God has guided my journey, and I know he guides others to me so I can help them. I wake every morning and tell Him what I am grateful for. Then I pray for Him to put people in my life who need me or I need them.

God does this daily. It is amazing the people who have started showing up in my life like Kimberly West; I thank God for her knowledge, inspiration and friendship daily. She is an amazing lady! I know he sends clients to me that need me on a daily basis. When you have been heavy all your life, many emotions need to be worked through. Since I can identify with that, I can help so many by showing compassion and diligence to get healthy. Plus I'm walking the walk while talking the talk to encourage one to love what they see in the mirror. Too many of us let the scale define us. It is just a number yet can be terrifying.

Getting to a healthy BMI is a journey for many of us, but I feel it is worth it to live a longer, healthier life. I want to help people live their lives not just exist because a whole world is waiting to be explored. I teach each client how to make a vision board and set short and long-term goals. Having visuals of what you are working towards can help keep you in line. Adding quotes and sayings continually make you think. "Nothing tastes as good as thin will feel" or "A minute on the lips, a lifetime on the hips" and my favorite "What you eat in private shows up in public." These can be read every morning to keep you on track. Look at the vision board daily. Make short five, ten or twenty pound goals depending on how much you have to lose. When you reach them go for a manicure or pedicure. A massage at fifty pounds lost is an amazing feeling. Getting new clothes, planning little trips, maybe a photo session, these are a few things that can really make you stay on target. One of my major things on my goal board was a twelve-day cruise to Greece that I get to book when I hit Onederland (meaning the one hundreds). Many obese people call it this because when you have been heavy for so long, it is hard to remember ever weighing less than two hundred pounds.

It seems like a dream. Every time I weighed in under a big number - five hundred, four hundred and so on - I would scream in victory, "GOODBYE!" I love receiving the celebration calls from clients. It always reinforces why I chose to become a health coach. More than one client calls me their 'life coach' because we are not dieting but working towards optimal health and changing our lifestyles. It is about more than health; it's dealing with emotions, day to day problems, history, and learned behaviors that create bad habits. People eat when they are sad, angry, happy or just bored. We have to learn to change these behaviors and sometimes it can be really challenging.

Much of our society celebrates birthdays, anniversaries and much more with food. When meeting with friends, everyone suggests lunch. What about meeting in the park to go for a walk or meet at your local gym to take a class. Water aerobics is a blast and even better with friends. Clients journal to get daily feelings on paper; it is a great release. It lets you document the journey so later you can see how you transformed your thoughts and changed habits. Many have told me that they have worked through many things by doing this and not keeping things bottled up inside because suppressing is not good for your health. Next we work on sleep habits. Getting quality sleep is important and plays a major part in our health. If you are not getting adequate sleep you won't lose weight. This is really hard for many people. Bad habits come into play, like staying up watching too much TV or playing on the computer. I suggest setting a bedtime so that you know you're getting six to eight hours of quality sleep, letting your body rejuvenate for the next day. It's also important to fuel your body correctly to boost your metabolism. To drive this point home, an analogy I like to use is it's like trying to drive from Florida to New York on one tank of fuel; your engine would stop.

HEALTHY TIPS TO LIVE BY

1) Leave home prepared: Bring water and meal replacements in case you are out longer than expected. Six small meals each day is part of the lifestyle.

2) Eat within a half-hour of waking: While this can include coffee, food, preferably a protein, is a necessity.

3) Keep Hydrated: Drink a minimum of eight, eight-ounce glasses of water. Better yet drink half your weight in ounces.

4) Exercise regularly: Doing just thirty minutes, three times a week will lengthen your life. Exercise is important for heart health and lowering blood sugar if diabetic.

Getting healthy is amazing. Never having had health or getting it back and making it happen is a true victory, one that is hard to describe and put into words. While it is amazing doing for you, helping others achieve success is truly fulfilling. Seeing them transform from unhealthy to healthy is life changing. It goes beyond what one can imagine. It's giving them back their health and a longer, more prosperous life.

I love my life. My weight no longer defines me. My love for God, my loving husband, family and others is what I'm about. Getting America healthy one person at a time allows my spirit and soul to soar. So my mind, body and soul are continually transforming with God's direction. If you are ready to join me, I'm only an email or phone call away. The time is now to get healthy. Don't let your weight hold you back from living!!!

Sisters **KAREN BINETTE-RAPPORT** and **LESLIE BRUCE** always dreamed of owning a business together but their individual careers had them going in separate directions. Only after years of professional and personal experiences, did the right business show up.

Originally from Boston, Leslie moved to California after graduating college, where she worked in various positions in the apparel industry. Through her range of experiences that included apparel manufacturing, retail buyer, running a sales organization and working for Levi Strauss & Co., she developed the skills and expertise that she now applies to running Feel the Hugs®.

During this time, Karen got married, became a mother of two, and taught physical education. Karen's personal experiences led her into the arena of fundraising. Later she would become a Regional Sales Director for a well-known publishing company working with schools.

Family support became more important than ever when Karen's husband was diagnosed with cancer. Both Karen and Leslie realized the amazing impact a simple hug can make to someone going through a tough time. And so, Feel the Hugs® was born. Knowing that people can't always be physically present to provide that all important hug, the sisters created a company that enables people to send "hugs" to anyone for any occasion, through their super cute t-shirts, teddy bears, and much more. In keeping with their mission statement, they donate a portion of all sales to cancer research.

Leslie and Karen are passionate about creating a "hug" movement with their unique products. Their positive attitude and enthusiasm make working together a true joy, and the responses they receive from hug recipients are their biggest reward. The hug sisters know the positive energy and connection of a hug helps to make the world a better place.

DEDICATION

A special thanks to our "angel" Adrianne who was the inspiration of the three little words scribbled on a cap. Although you are not with us anymore, we know you are smiling down upon us, and we know you still "Feel the Hugs®"!

Chapter Three

Two Sisters, One Vision: Feel the Hugs®

Written by Leslie Bruce and Karen Binette Rapport as told by Leslie Bruce

Trust that the universe has a plan for you. It did for us. But you must first try something......Let us explain.....

TWO PEOPLE COULD NOT BE MORE DIFFERENT.

As kids, my older sister, by 3 1/2 years, Karen tortured me with spiders - she dangled them in front of my eyes until I screamed so loud that our parents would run down the hallway and break us up. She teased me, bribed me, cut my hair off and sprayed my girl-friend's hair silver, and her mother never wanted her to play at our house again. She was a terror!! Then sibling magic happened once I turned 18 and we became best friends. We are opposite in so many ways. We look nothing alike; in fact, she convinced me I was ad-opted. She is a carefree slob and I am neat and organized; she is bold and vivacious, and I am shy and reserved. Yet we are so in tune with each other's thoughts that we even finish each other's sentences.

For years we thought it would be fun to work together. Well Karen did, I really wasn't too sure. For about twenty-five years we batted around mostly zany ideas, none of which were serious enough to consider, except perhaps for the patterned knee braces to match tennis outfits!! Besides, we both had successful careers and lived 3000 miles apart. Eventually a series of trying events led us to the concept of Feel the Hugs®.

Karen had a friend named Adrianne who was dying from lung cancer. She bought a white cap from Walmart and scribbled the words "Feel the Hugs" on it. Adrianne was really touched, and said, "Karen, I *FEEL* them." The expression was also one she used with her kids long distance on the phone. It really is amazing if you close your eyes and put your intention on it, you really can "feel" that feeling. Little did we know those three little words would impact us so.

Shortly thereafter we had a conversation that would remain in our memories forever. Karen's husband was diagnosed with stage IV kidney cancer and she was scared. Thoughts of being alone and financially challenged plagued her. She wanted to work again yet had limitations. Karen asked me, what if we use that expression, "Feel the Hugs," and create a business? It was the first time in about 20 years I didn't laugh her off and said it might have merit. We put in motion a plan to test our idea. Our original concept was focused on warming the heart of a patient in a hospital so that they could "feel" the hugs of their family and friends all the time. We also wanted to develop a character with our logo to represent our new business that would be warm yet whimsical. We could see it in our heads but neither of us is great artists. Somehow the universe put the people in our path that we needed and things fell into place.

It's amazing when you put the intention out in the universe how circumstances happen. No one shows up by accident. My husband Bob and I had been planning a vacation to North Carolina to check out some places we thought we might like to move to. The day before we left for our trip, I was talking on the phone to my girlfriend from high school, and she mentioned that her sister Judy, a talented artist, lived in North Carolina. She suggested we give her a call, and we made plans to get together while we were there. What we thought would be coffee for an hour or so in the afternoon turned into an amazing visit. Six hours later we were still talking and laughing over dinner! Judy understood exactly what we wanted in our character. She is even more whimsical than we are and was in tune with our vision right away. Now here's a bit of irony.....My nephew, David, was born with a birth anomaly, missing fingers and toes. Karen has always had a thing about hands because of it, and she didn't want fingers on our character. Interestingly enough our artist Judy was also born missing fingers! Amazing coincidence? We think not!

Twenty-nine years ago when David was born, Rabbi Harold Kushner author of *When Bad Things Happen to Good People* went to visit Karen in the hospital. He had a profound message that resonates to this day. He told her, "Your life has changed and you will meet many people you normally would not meet and do many things you normally would not do because of your son." Starting a foundation for children like David, called Helping Hands, never would have been created, nor would years of fundraising for Children's Hospital Boston where David was treated. Now in retrospect, we can see this business probably would not have been created, and we would not have met all the amazing people that have crossed our path. To say things happen for a reason certainly is true for us.

Our character, Arely, was born in September, 2008. He is a happy soul with a positive message, terrific energy, and he always hugs a heart. The name Arely was found one evening while my sister and I were talking long distance, and searching the internet for interesting names. The name Arely is both masculine and feminine and it means brave, courageous, and heroic. We believe it represents so many people be it soldiers, firemen, patients in hospitals or kids going off to school for the first time! It was a perfect fit.

Arely also plays an important role on our website. We came up with the idea of "Where's Arely?" because we wanted people to wear our t-shirts all over the world and take pictures to put on our website. It has been so much fun to see the pictures from distant and exotic places as Arely continues to spread his good energy around the world. Our business began to take shape as each piece of the puzzle fell into place.

The beginning of the business was a challenge to be sure. At the time, I lived outside of San Francisco, while Karen was in Florida. I had a background in the apparel business and therefore developed the organizational aspect of the business, while Karen focused on selling product and getting our vision out to the South Florida market. Feel the Hugs® showed up at neighborhood walks, through speeches in various communities, and at hospitals. Our little t-shirt business was ready to grow. It was difficult, to say the least, to work on opposite coasts. So at just this time, my husband decided to take early retirement and we were searching for a place to move in North Carolina. We never envisioned ourselves living in Florida, but decided if we were going to give this business our full effort we needed to be near each other.

Karen developed dystonia at age 50. It's a disease that affects her eyes; they want to shut. We had to live nearby as she cannot drive more than the mile and a half it takes to get from her house to mine. So we put our trust in the vision and we moved forward. While the foundation of our company was established, we knew that working closely together would drive our vision into a dynamic business. We wanted to provide a novel way to create connections. People would have the ability to wrap themselves in a hug sent from a loved one.

My husband and I drove the 3000 miles across the country with our dog headed for a new chapter in our lives. For us, it was a huge step to take after living in California for over 30 years. Everyone still asks us why did you leave California?!!! Change sometimes has blessings attached to it. Our parents are in their mid 80's, also living in Florida, and once again after many years we are all together again.

My husband used to tell me all the time to just try something whenever I was stuck or not sure what to do, and in this case it applied to starting our business. If you try something and it doesn't work out, it could lead to something else. And that something could lead to the "right" thing. If it doesn't work out, it doesn't mean you failed, it just means you should try something else. We learned so many lessons through the process of starting our business. *Just try something* was a big one.

TURNING THE "BIG C" INTO A "C" OF HUGS. CAN YOU SEE IT?!

One of the things we learned through our experience was that cancer envelops the entire family, not just the patient. Creating Feel the Hugs took on even more importance as a way to keep Karen focused on positive things and off the disease and the what-ifs. So I emailed Karen projects and ideas daily and we talked about business and not the C-word.

During this time the nurses at Sylvester Comprehensive Cancer Center in Florida where Karen was now spending a great deal of time, were extremely supportive and even let us know that our business concept was on the right track. This eventually led to our first "Feel the Hugs day" where the nurses and staff wore our t-shirts and together we spread hugs and happiness throughout the hospital. It was a day of staff camaraderie and team building and of course lots of hugs. The patients received more hugs than usual. The staff smiled even brighter as pictures clicked all day. And through our product sales that day we helped raise money for the hospital. If we could create good energy there just imagine how great it would be to create it everywhere. As we left the hospital that day, we were so inspired that this could be the beginning of our "hug movement." We remembered someone saying to us years ago....."if it doesn't exist create it!" So we did!

"Make every day a reason to Celebrate" Karen Binette Rapport

If you look at the definition of a hug in the dictionary you would read words like: cherish or cling to; embrace self; congratulate or be pleased with self; comfort, console; to express affection.

All of these words define what Feel the Hugs is about. As we showed our concept to our friends and family they all affirmed our idea and took it one level further. Hugs are necessary for everyone for good occasions as well as tough ones. Parents could literally wrap their kids in their hugs as they go off to camp or school, and girlfriends could send far away friends "hugs" when they can't be with them on a special day. Grandparents could send their grand-kids hugs to show them their love, and veterans and soldiers are always in need of a hug....the list is endless.

We heard a story of grandparents who sent their grandchildren t-shirts and then they would Skype each other at night wearing their tees to say good night so everyone would Feel the Hugs from each other. Our shirts were also used as a connection between a mother and daughter who lost their husband and dad but lived on opposite coasts. They put their shirts on and talked on the phone feeling both their own hugs and the loving energy of their husband/dad. We have seen happy tears, sad tears and know that healing happens in so many ways.

Another woman bought shirts for her entire family who was planning a surprise birthday party for her sister. Everyone wore Feel the Hugs t-shirts so when she walked into the room, she could feel the energy of a huge family hug. Then they wrapped the guest of honor in her own Feel The Hugs® t-shirt in her favorite color. The family is planning to use their shirts every year for their family reunions.

And then there is this touching testimonial of our friend Deb who tells us whenever she has a bad day she goes into her room to put on one of her many hug shirts so she can Feel the Hugs® and immediately feels better.

What we first envisioned grew before our eyes. We inherently knew hugs felt good but through research we came to know that science proves that hugs are actually good for your health. A hormone called oxytocin is raised in the body which has a calming effect, reduces stress and lowers blood pressure, thereby helping to protect us from heart disease. Hugs create connections, give a sense of belonging, and help build self-esteem. We discovered that you need a minimum of eight hugs a day just to be, and 12 hugs a day to thrive. Hugs should be heart to heart (left side to left side) so you can feel that *heart energy* between each person. Hugs convey all sorts of messages from friendship to comfort to love.

We became hug experts of a sort, learning more and more about the positive effects of hugs. Hugs are healing too, and we want to share all that we know through what we coined our "Hug Movement." Whenever we walk into a room people now say, "There are the Hug Sisters!" It took our branding one step further.

At this time in our lives we never envisioned we would be reinventing ourselves with another career and starting a new business. It was important for us in the second chapter of our lives to create a business where we have a positive impact and feel good going to work every day.

Our belief is everyone wants to feel connected. Our business facilitates the connection of people, and creates joyfulness, peace, and kindness. Because cancer played such an important role in the beginning of our business and we saw how it affected the lives of our family and others, we created our mission statement to include that we would donate a portion of all sales to cancer research.

There have been more than a few times we have been frustrated....running a business takes lots of time and lots of work. Patience is huge especially when two opposite people are working so closely together! We both made big sacrifices to get the business moving. As we look at what we have achieved in the past two years, we are amazed about what two people can accomplish. We run all aspects of a company including merchandising, operations, product development, researching trademarks, accounting, PR, sales, marketing, tags, brochures, every word, every picture, every Facebook post, social media, website operations, order fulfillment, event bookings, and on and on. We take classes to learn many of the things we don't know. We don't have enough hours in a day to do all the things we want to do. Many mentors have told us that we are on the right path, just do the work and the rewards will follow. When we got our first responses from people who gave our products as gifts we knew we were on the right track and we were convinced that the "feeling" we were creating was really special. One of our friends gave our "Feel the Hugs" teddy bear to someone in the hospital, and as he opened the present he burst into tears of joy. Our friend received such heartfelt thanks from him that she cried tears of joy as well. Then the story came back to us and we felt the hugs come full circle. This and so many stories like it inspire us to persevere and push through the trying times.

And what's the next step? Our goal is to bring Arely to life through a series of children's books. Arely will teach children positive messages, values and that happiness is a choice.

We hope Arely will be every child's best friend and they will emulate his warmth and kind-heartedness. We believe in the magic of Arely!

We love what we do!!! And we are passionate about our hug movement. We know how vital hugs are and want others to truly understand the importance of hugs for your body and soul. We both witnessed the impact of how hugs are healing when a woman we met was going in to the hospital extremely nervous, unsure of what lay ahead. Her husband purchased her a Feel the Hugs t-shirt in a vibrant color, which she immediately put on and came back to us beaming, grateful for the support. We know we are making a difference and know we have touched many hearts. Our dream is to touch many, many more.

LESSONS FROM THE HUG SISTERS

Little did we know our kaleidoscope of life was the roadmap to where we are today. In looking back, we realize all of our personal and professional experiences, the highs and lows in life, and over forty years of combined sales background was the training ground for where we are today. We've learned so much, grown spiritually, and loved helping others create their success too! We hope the wisdom we gained can help others use what worked for us.

CHANNELING ARELY

People often ask us how we are so upbeat all the time. We believe in and use affirmations daily. Developing a positive mindset is a powerful tool for happiness and success. Replacing any negative thoughts with short positive statements, repeated over and over again, is the way this is done; these are called affirmations. Positive affirmations reprogram thought patterns and if used continually positive changes start to happen. It is important to use affirmations in the present tense. Saying "I will"....means you will someday in the future, but not now. Always phrase your words in the NOW. I am.... I have....I choose, etc. and repeat the affirmations with faith and conviction. Some examples of affirmations are: I choose to make positive healthy choices in my life......and I deserve to be happy and successful. Put your affirmations in writing and recite them many times daily. You can put them on post-it notes all around the house. Say your affirmations with passion! They can really change your mind set. Anytime the negativity creeps in, stop it and change the words.

Before we go to a meeting or an event we say some of our favorite affirmations to inspire a great outcome. For example, "Everything and everyone prospers us now" is a favorite. Surround yourself with positive words and positive people and things that make you happy. Remember, "I think I can, I think I can, I know I can, I know I can....." What a great affirmation! You really can make the shift in your life to positivity by using affirmations.

Affirmations are very similar to creative visualization. Together they are powerful tools. Do you have a vision of what your future looks like? We made a vision board for our office allowing us to constantly see images of where we want to be in our lives and what we want to accomplish. It's a really fun process to do, simply by cutting out images and words from magazines and pasting them to a poster board. It may include pictures of a beautiful beach, a place you want to live, the type of car you want to drive, positive words, calming thoughts, anything that makes you happy or that you want in your lives. On ours are words such as prosperous, abundance, happiness, creative, kindness, healthy, generosity, laughter, and even Donny Deutsch......really? Actually he is someone we aspire to have a meeting with and think he is a brilliant marketer - so, why not?

What you dream you can achieve, ask and you shall receive, are all great positive sayings we have heard over and over. When you use a vision board the images and words enter your subconscious brain, and send a message to the universe of your desires. When we walk by our board one particular message usually resonates that we can focus on for the day.

Years ago I made a vision board and included all sorts of images on it including a beautiful kitchen. The board was in a closet and moved with us from house to house. One day, years later, when I pulled it out, I noticed the kitchen I had in the new house we were living in was the same as the one in the picture on my old vision board!!! Manifest what you want in your life! You will be amazed at what happens! Remember, *just try something.*

DO YOU DREAD THE SALES CALL?

All too often we meet solo-preneurs who may have a great product or idea or business but the fear of sales holds them back.

Sales do not need to be scary. It's a numbers game. You have to remember it's not personal when someone says no. The Colonel (KFC) made over 1000 sales calls before he found a restaurant that would partner with him. Walt Disney had a rough start to his career when he was fired by a newspaper editor because he "lacked imagination and had no good ideas." Everyone fears failure. But if you can look at failure as an opportunity to learn, it becomes a positive process. Each NO gets you closer to YES. We look at sales calls as an opportunity to meet new friends. After all, sales are all about relationships. People like to do business with people they know, like, and trust. Be likable, be authentic, and be honest. Bring that huggability factor into your business life too!

It's also important to be thoroughly knowledgeable on your product or business, and practice, practice, practice what you want to say before you meet with any client. Be prepared for any objections, and know your competition. Know how you can be of service to a potential customer, and how you can satisfy their needs. Sometimes people feel like they are being a pest, and therefore wait to make a call, or don't make the call at all. Change the belief of being a pest into one of being of service. And you can even preface the conversation with, "I don't want to be a pest, but...."

All too often, people spend too much time on busy work procrastinating before making sales. It's the face to face, or phone contact that makes a sale. Don't put it off one moment longer. It's never going to be perfect. If you take too long to think about it, you won't do it!! Take the first step. *Just try something.*

Sales are not made sitting in the office. It really is true that a body at rest stays at rest. One year when I was at a sales meeting for Levi Strauss & Co., they demonstrated a simple message that has stayed with me for years. Before the meeting began someone taped a one dollar bill underneath a chair and then told the audience to get up and look underneath their seats. Someone found the one dollar bill of course......the message being "You have to get off your butt to make a buck."!! Simple and very effective.

One day we were running a work errand at the mall and on our way out stopped at Marmi, a well known shoe store. Who can resist shoes??! We were both wearing our "tattoos," the Feel the Hugs® t-shirts, and once again it sparked conversation. Little did we know that we happened to be talking to the regional manager and she loved the concept of our business. The store manager was planning a special event that weekend, but the details were still up in the air. It was no coincidence that we appeared in her store when she needed us. They asked us if we could do a trunk show with them a couple of days later. As it happened, the Midwest had just suffered tremendous loss during a series of tornadoes and we thought it appropriate to partner with them and use this event to raise money for the Red Cross for the tornado victims. I was hesitant about a last minute event, being the perfectionist that I am. We need to plan, can I put everything together so quickly, would we be prepared, and on and on!! If we had waited until we were fully prepared, we would have missed the window of opportunity. Karen said let's go, so we did!! At the event the store personnel wore our shirts, it changed up the energy, and we met some incredible people that day! We created a win-win by raising money for the Red Cross, new customers came in to the store, we spread our message to more people, we created lots of new huggers, and we had FUN! And Karen bought shoes!

You have to get out and meet people! Join a networking group; they are a great way to connect with people. We joined several networking groups, especially women-oriented groups where our new circle of supportive women were like-minded, caring, and ready to help each other learn and to promote each other. We attended many meetings and learned networking was not just about passing out business cards and screaming "buy my stuff." It was getting to know people on a personal level. We have met so many people who have become friends and customers. Many mentors have mentioned that you should always treat everyone as if they are "the one." You never know who could be your next customer or who could connect you to the person you need to meet.

KNOW THAT YOU ARE NEVER TOO OLD TO REINVENT YOURSELF!

Karen and I had been out of the corporate world for a while and learned that you really need to keep your brain engaged. The sharpness we once had faded a bit, perhaps part of it was aging, but we quickly learned we needed to read, learn and constantly grow. Years back when we were both working for large corporations, we were well-trained, but today the challenges are more complex and technology changes so quickly, social media entered the arena, and blogs and tweets and oh gosh.....business changed as we knew it. How do you keep up with it all?

What we do love about social media is that we have formed more new relationships. In fact, we made many Facebook "friends" and when we finally meet them face to face, (more hugs of course!) it is like meeting someone we have known for a long time.

Remember you are always selling yourself along with the products and services you are selling your customers. Your reputation is everything. When the sale is complete, it's not really over! That's when follow-up and customer service comes into play. Be outstanding! Superior customer service will generate repeat business and referral sales.

WHAT DO YOU DO WHEN YOU ARE BLOCKED?

We meet a lot of individuals trying to make a go of a business. We both worked from home for a large portion of our careers and know what that's like. It has been beneficial in many ways that we are working together even though we are opposites! We LOVE brainstorming sessions and we bounce ideas off of each other all the time. It's a time to throw out all kinds of ideas, without regard to practicality. For whatever topic you are brainstorming, list on paper every idea that comes to mind quickly. Afterward you can go back over them and see what resonates, and what ideas you would like to implement. You need to respect each other's ideas no matter how crazy they may sound. It takes work when each has strong opinions. Remembering your mission statement and goals can always bring you back to center.

Everyone needs some sort of support system whether it is a coach, a networking group, a spouse you can bounce ideas off of, or someone you trust. The beauty of a partner or mentor is once you have a product or thought, you have a sounding board to test the idea and see if there is value in it. We have learned you cannot go it totally alone. If you work out of an office or home you need to get out of it often!! We get stuck a lot and find that just going to Panera or Starbucks for coffee changes the energy as we interact with people and get the creativity moving again. When you are alone it's easy to get stuck and make excuses and go under the covers. The power of two can really help; when one is down the other helps to pull her up.

One day we were working in a coffee shop before a meeting and our teddy bear was on the table and a woman stopped by to ask us about it. Guess what? We ended up mailing a gift to her friend! Take props with you or conversation starters when you are out, be it a book you wrote or a brochure about your business or something bright and bold to grab attention. You may meet someone who is your ideal client or a new friend!

Sometimes we find going to the beach or getting out in nature gets the creative juices going again. For some people, it's putting on some beautiful music, for others its singing as loud as you can to a musical! Every time we see a rainbow we both simultaneously burst into a chorus of "Somewhere over the Rainbow" totally off key but laughing the whole time. Change up the energy in any way you enjoy!

The other way to get unblocked is to become quiet. Ahhh, ohm-hug time. Meditate. We are by no means experts on meditation but we know it works! Meditation is a powerful tool. By spending some quiet alone time, meditation can help unlock creative potential, reduce stress, and clear mental clutter. Meditation can help when you have feelings of being overwhelmed too. There are so many benefits to meditation that countless books have been written on the subject. Taking time for meditation is like wrapping yourself in a big bear hug.

Find a quiet space where you won't be interrupted. It does not matter if it is inside or outside. Sometimes being outside creates a natural calmness. Try the ocean, listening to a gentle breeze in your backyard, by a lake or water feature, wherever you are comfortable. If it is hard to quiet your mind, you can try a guided meditation CD.

Not everyone can sit still for 15-20 minutes, which is why we love active meditation. This can be running, swimming, or walking, any activity where you focus on body, mind and spirit.

The important thing is to try it! *Just try something!*

One of the blocks we all run into is the naysayers. No matter what, they will make a negative comment, or try to steal your enthusiasm. Don't let them block you or your wonderful ideas!! Negative people compete for energy and thus for power. They have to steal someone else's energy to feel powerful. Positivity is so much stronger than negativity, so when you encounter negative people just shoot them back with love!

When you get blocked, remember *just try something*; it could lead to the "right" thing.

AND WHAT DOES GRATITUDE HAVE TO DO WITH ANY OF THIS?

If you begin the day with gratitude, being thankful, you can set the tone for a glorious day. Focusing on gratitude makes it grow. Once we shift energy and begin to have gratitude we bring more of what we want into our lives. Gratitude is a magnet. Once you focus on gratitude, it's impossible to be angry or down because gratitude redirects your mind from the negative to the positive. It helps to keep peace in your life. We practice gratitude all the time by celebrating small milestones or big achievements. We are always grateful for the kind words people say to us and love the unsolicited testimonials we receive from recipients of our products. Do you see the glass half empty or half full? Do you think of the things you don't have or are you grateful for the things you do have? Shift your thinking to all the things you are thankful for and watch your life turn around. Practice adding gratitude to your life daily.

Be grateful for other people's successes as well. It's easy to become envious and think "what about me?" The law of cause and effect states "any action creates an equal and opposite reaction." Some people call it karma. So, if like attracts like then it only follows that by being happy for other people's successes, you will attract the same into your life. There is so much abundance in the universe, and enough for everyone, so show support, happiness, and gratefulness to others and you will attract the same back.

Both of us believe work doesn't have to be so serious. So much of the day is filled with work that fun and laughter should be part of the journey. Don't take everything so seriously! Make sure to add laughter and light and HUGS to your day.

FEEL YOURSELF HUGGED WITH THESE TEN TIPS

Just try something!

Lighten up!! don't take things so seriously

Celebrate your accomplishments

Meditate

Hang around like minded positive people

Use affirmations daily

Be authentic, let your personality shine through
in whatever you do

Practice gratitude

Don't go it alone, get a support system

Hug every day!

This entire book is written to trust the voice within. You can be anything you want to be; you can accomplish anything you want to achieve. You just have to be authentic and true and trust the little inner voice.

Is there a point when you finally know it all? When you reach your goal? When all the lessons have been learned? It's not about reaching an end......it's the joy of the journey. *Just try something.*

Both Karen and I finally found the little voice within. It has a big message.....Wherever you are, Feel the Hugs®.

*Feel the Hugs® and our character Arely are registered trademarks. All rights reserved.

ALLISON TURNER truly exemplifies what it is to live a holistic life, bringing over 20 years of experience to her practice and sharing the simple secrets to creating a life based on one's true desires and authentic self, while incorporating mind, body and spiritual practices. Through a long and successful career of playing and then coaching tennis, Allison discovered that her true passion and talent was in encouraging and coaching individuals to know that anything was possible both on the court and in their lives! As a gifted photographer with a strong connection to being in nature, Allison has created a line of photo prints and post cards which reflect her artistry in finding meaning for your own life through the perfection in nature.

Allison is known as a "Visionary" as she works with individuals or groups to guide them along the Pathway to Mind and Spirit during times of discontent, transition or expansion to new heights. She presents to her audiences with a warm heart, focused intention and clarity of purpose, ensuring you get what you need to grow and expand.

In addition, she has joined forces with Allow Your Spirit to Soar to accept the divinely appointed position of Vice President. They offer LIVE "Spirit & Vision Shops", By Invitation Only 2-Day Retreats, Destination Journeys, Tele-Seminars, Memberships for your personal and business life and individual & group coaching.

Allison Turner, M.B.A.

Phone: (773) 991-3111

For more information:

www.PathwaytoMindandSpirit.com

www.AllowYourSpiritToSoar.com

DEDICATION

I dedicate these chapters to my aunt, Jeanne LaDuke, and my friend who is like a sister to me, Jean Feit, who lead by quiet example. To Kim Wheeler who inspires me to see the possibilities. To Nancy Matthews who helps me realize my dreams. To Kimberly West, my partner, who accepts me for who I am and allows me to embrace emotions in a big way. Each of you believe in me, play an important role in my life and allow me to live in faith; for that, I am grateful!

Chapter Four

Letting Go:

Walking the Path of Faith
by Allison Turner

When I was honored with the request to be part of this book, I was excited to be able to share my story in the hope that others who feel stuck in their lives will experience a sense of freedom and possibilities. While it took me, what seems like a lifetime to get to this place where I now embrace the passion and excitement of my journey and vision, I have also come to recognize that all my experiences up until now make me who I am today. I have always been on a journey to realize my higher calling and greater purpose in the world but it took the death of my long-time boyfriend in 2007 to really spark that energy and make me never say 'no' again. I made a conscious decision that I wanted no regrets in life and I was willing to do whatever it took to accomplish that. I slowly learned to listen to my inner voice, which you may call intuition or Divine Guidance but it took time because I had to reprogram the way I thought, felt, and embraced my life. I had to release the need to continually control or script every aspect of my life and trust that I will get where I want to go by continuing to embrace my strengths, let go of my limiting beliefs and live into my life's vision. I had to live a life of faith.

"The Voice" is in each one of us if we choose to listen and really connect with what we feel and believe our true calling is, for the short time we are on Earth. Many of us choose to ignore that voice in order to stay on the "safe" path. Some people learn early in life to listen to that inner calling and they feel the support in living their purpose and that is a true gift. Others have chosen a life that does not make them really happy but perhaps makes another person happy. We are responsible for the choices we make in our lives. Our vision for our lives connects us to our purpose and higher calling. It is the "why" for our lives. It is the reason we get up in the morning and live in that place of excitement and awe for another new day filled with possibilities. It is the reason that we visualize a greater way of living and contributing to our world. When we live by trusting "the voice" inside, our lives start to fall into place and we come from a place of peace and passion instead of fear and frustration. We live our journey and realize that nothing is impossible because we believe in our vision and embrace the path where it leads.

When you have ignored "the voice" inside for such a long period of time, it is hard to break that pattern and really listen because fear immediately shows up. Listening to "the voice" inside requires us to step out of our comfort zone and embrace love and change. When we are comfortable, we may feel content but not really passionate and excited about our lives. I made a conscious decision that I want to experience that passion and excitement in my life even if I must experience the fear and frustration along the way. I am willing to embrace the whole spectrum of emotions because I have found that in order to live into my calling and embrace the passion and excitement that comes with that, I have to acknowledge, embrace and walk through the fear that continually shows up. I accept that living my vision and trusting "the voice" inside of me far outweighs the challenges I encounter and the limiting beliefs I have about myself. I have learned to trust in the journey and live in faith.

One of the last heart-wrenching statements my boyfriend said to me was, "You have to let me go." Looking into his eyes, I saw the culmination of pain that I couldn't even fathom. The whites of his eyes were a jaundiced yellow color streaked with red. His cheek bones were protruding creating larger than life eyes. Until that moment when I heard his request, only nine days before his death, I never knew the intensity of the pain. That statement penetrated into my soul and still resonates with me several years later. It spoke directly to my need to keep him alive as long as possible instead of letting him go. What I learned during his last days was that life in that moment was not about me. I had to let go so he could complete his earthly journey; I had to let go of the fear of losing him and trust that his soul would continue on its journey and I too would continue on my path. Although sadness and grief were inevitable, I chose to embrace the important lesson of letting go and living in faith.

Our life's journey is not so much about us but about the individuals we have the opportunity to impact in a wonderful way. As I have walked this journey, I have learned that control no longer serves me. I felt stuck in my life for many years because I tried to maintain control. I sought control over my emotions because the fear of taking any risk and following the voice inside was overpowering. I had not been able to follow my voice for so long; I had to learn to embrace the possibilities that came with listening intently and acting. When I shied away from experiencing the fear and pain, I also limited the ability to really embrace the passion and excitement. Any time I sense myself trying to "control" a situation, I have learned that I have to release that need and walk in faith. Faith requires me to be centered, grounded and trust in my greater purpose as it unfolds. Life unfolds one step at a time so it is important to listen and act as these steps are slowly revealed. We often don't understand or see the greater picture but are called to have faith as we live into our greater purpose.

As I continued the journey to live into my vision, I realized that the job I had, which had served me well for a long time, no longer held any real passion. When I set the date to walk away from the job having no real plan other than to live into my vision for my life, I felt a sense of peace. Setting this date seven months in advance forced me to let go of the need to control everything. It affirmed my need to trust not only my intuition but the fact that a greater plan existed for me. I emphasize that not everything has been easy. As the date of departure got closer, I started second guessing my decision. When I finally resigned and was offered a leave of absence for the summer followed by a part-time job, it took everything I had to say 'no this is not what I am called to do.' The part-time job offered me a safety net that was enticing and that in the past I would have taken in a heartbeat. This time was different because I listened to my intuition and knew that this was not the path I was called to walk. My journey has not been easy because I didn't flip the switch one day and say from this day forward, I will live by listening to my intuition, letting go of that need to control everything and having faith that when I do this everything will work out for the best. Unfortunately life isn't that simple. My journey was influenced by my daily thoughts, the people around me and my history. In letting go of my "safe" job, I started the journey to let go of the fear, the belief that I am not good enough, and the constant need to second guess my intuition by overanalyzing everything. Previously I had ignored my voice and over thought decisions in regards to my tennis playing, career choices and even a simple conversation. What if I said or did the wrong thing? What would the repercussions be? In reality, I was losing out by not following my intuition.

One of my greatest challenges continues to be breaking the bonds of my own negative thoughts because our thoughts control our emotions and our actions. I have learned that they aren't my thoughts but words from others in my life over the course of the years. I have also learned that I must surround myself with positive, life-giving people who support me for who I am and the path I am leading. People like this can be hard to find initially but as I walk further down the path, I attract them to me. Again I return to my boyfriend's pleading request, "You have to let me go." Today I hear those words in my head and they remind me that some things are simply not in our control and we have to trust that if we are truly following our purpose that all will work out how it is supposed to work out. This belief, which seems so simple, is not so easy in reality and for me it has been a constant challenge.

Pathway to Mind and Spirit, Inc. was born out of this work. I came to realize that the more I tried to control and get stuck in my fears and negativity, the less I liked my life, the less I liked myself. I wasn't truly happy and I didn't love what I did or love myself. It wasn't how I envisioned making a difference in the world. My career had served me well for the past few years, but everyone should have the opportunity to live their life with passion, excitement and purpose. When you wake up in the morning, feeling that today is the same as yesterday and no different from tomorrow, you start to wonder where the possibilities went. What happened to the dreams? It isn't about waiting for happiness but embracing happiness. It's about connecting with others and knowing that each of us can impact another human being in a positive way through a simple 'hello' and smile. It's about treating everyone and everything in the world as part of the Divine because every living thing is created in the likeness of God. It's about loving what you do on a daily basis in every moment; it is creating a vision for your life and walking that path of purpose. My calling is to help others live into their highest potential, to create a vision for their lives and to embrace them as a spiritual being destined to leave the world a better place than when they were born. Achieving this requires living a conscious life, connecting to one's Divinity and creating practices that continue to nourish the body, mind and spirit.

EMBRACING MY PATH

Walking this journey has required me to connect more and more to my spiritual side and my own divinity. I have learned to trust my intuition even when it leads me into unchartered territories that are frightening and scary. I now know and embrace that I am made in the likeness of the Creator and that my intuition is really God speaking through me and moving me along my path of purpose and calling me into my greatness. As I struggled in my previous career, feeling caged with no way out, the very clear message came to me that I didn't need to wait for the perfect moment to walk away. I already had that and simply needed to embrace it. Being able not only to hear but to live this message is accepting my intuition as my divine voice moving me forward on my path.

I continually work on my connection to spirit because I always remember that I have God within and am part of a greater world and I feel that connection to people. Every person is created in the likeness of the Divine and gives us an opportunity to create closer connections to God and the world. I believe our souls inhabit our earthly bodies and I long to have that soul connection with others. Our soul is what gives us the ability to embrace our purpose and want to leave the Earth a better place than when we came. The longer I walk this path, the more in tune I am to my energy and the energy surrounding me and I seek out and embrace the soul connection with another spiritual being.

Walking this spiritual path leaves me very vulnerable to another person's energy which is sometimes wonderful and sometimes draining. When we walk into the world and encounter someone who is upbeat, energized and passionate, we pick up that energy and it uplifts us; when we encounter someone who is negative or rude to us, we pick up that energy as well. When I feel the negative energy and need to re-center and re-align my energy to stay balanced, nature is very important to me. When I am feeling out of touch with my soul, I go to nature to re-connect to God and the greater good in the world. I can spend a couple of hours on the beach listening to the waves, smelling the salt air, watching the seagulls, pelicans, and sandpipers as they fly or scurry around in the sand and it gives me a sense of calm. As I gaze across the Atlantic Ocean, I wonder what people on another continent are doing at this very moment. I sense their energy and connect to the power of human potential which drives me to make the world a better place.

In walking this path I like to capture the perfection of nature through digital photography. While I believe that we cannot truly capture perfection, I do believe that we can continually appreciate and be grateful for what Mother Earth and God have provided to us. When I walk out my door, I am forever grateful as I gaze into the sky, smell a flower, or stare out over the massive ocean because I know all is right with the world.

Photography is a form of meditation for me. It inspires me to capture and share the best of Mother Nature. It inspires me to create and embrace the path I want to walk; it inspires me to greatness. In creating just the right picture, I look at something from as many sides as possible. I explore what else is around that might impact the scene in a positive way. I explore the possibilities looking for just the right fit in that moment. So while I have taken a couple of photography classes, I have no real formal training as a photographer but I largely operate by instinct. I see nature or an image of nature as a metaphor for life. I ask what it can teach us about ourselves and the world at large. What can a simple image share with me that I need to know? What can I share with others? I am so in tune with the contrast of the light and darkness, the spectrum of colors, and the energy of nature that it's very hard to see the world from a black and white perspective. This concept has challenged me to be open to experiencing life off the beaten path. I now look for the path less travelled; I seek to see situations from all angles until my intuition tells me the direction I am supposed to go. Yes, fear still plays a role in my life and challenges me to overcome my limiting beliefs because I know that life is so much greater. I experience the passion and life-giving energy of nature as I walk out the door each day. That is the experience I want in my life through my career, my play, my spirit, and my relationships. It is what I insist on having!

RIDING THE EMOTIONAL ROLLER COASTER

When I committed to my vision and created Pathway to Mind and Spirit, Inc., I embraced an emotional roller coaster that has yet to let up. What I didn't realize at the time was walking my path of passion and excitement in helping others live into their purpose, find their higher calling and connect to the divine world in a greater way, forced me to embrace a spectrum of emotions and really key into what my intuition is telling me to do. It has been a tough journey that I have continued to embrace and love; I sometimes liken it to being in therapy because every insecurity, fear, and limiting belief has shown up to complement my journey. Although it has been tough, I have loved every minute of it! Sometimes the intuitive side of me doesn't let up and challenges me to walk a path that I have not yet walked. It may simply be a new direction or a new opportunity but the challenge often brings up fears. I use the metaphor of climbing mountains where you finally get to the top and realize a cliff awaits you and the only way to forge ahead is to jump off that cliff. To take my life to the next level, I must step off the cliff and embrace the challenges ahead. I have learned to embrace the fears and challenges and step off the cliff in faith.

I have learned that when I am experiencing discomfort, I am in the midst of a growing process that will launch me to a greater level; I am on the path to creating a new comfort zone for my life. Many of us find one comfort zone in our lives and stay there. A comfort zone is a place that is safe, that presents few emotional challenges, and leaves you always wishing for more. Maybe you like where you are but you don't LOVE where you are. You aren't PASSIONATE about what you are doing. You don't experience EXCITEMENT in your life. But instead of experiencing the fear you back off and decide the life you have is better than facing the fear. At this stage in my journey, if I am too comfortable for too long, I question what is going on and really seek that next level in my life. I look for the growth opportunity and seek that next cliff to jump from so I continue to grow and experience more through relationships and situations. I seem to instinctually do this and I have learned that the journey up the mountain allows me to build the support system and relationships that I need to make this next jump. Instead of letting fear dictate what I do and force me into decisions that limit my journey, I have learned to trust the voice inside and let go of the need to control the situation.

Most recently, I was struggling with a situation and I felt the nervous, controlling energy coursing through my body, leaving me exhausted and frustrated. I knew that I had to release that energy and allow the situation to naturally unfold without being so attached to the outcome. When I went for a walk in the predawn hours, I asked the Universe for guidance and the answer came as the clouds in the sky cleared. Two words, 'patience' and 'trust' were clear. My own voice knew the answer all the time but I simply had to stop and listen. In times past, the fear would paralyze me and leave me stuck in a situation that was not the best for me. It kept me in one place. You may ask if I have ever regretted following my intuition and the answer is NO. Sometimes life does not turn out the way we hope but if we take no risks, we never experience the joy and possibilities that may show up.

WALKING IN FAITH

Faith has been difficult for me in the past because it required me to trust that all would work out for the best. Today, it requires me to walk through the fear and yell, "Thank you for showing up but I am no longer letting you control me."

I am still reminded about situations when life has not happened as I would have hoped when following my intuition and living in faith. When my boyfriend was diagnosed with cancer, after we had just moved to South Florida welcoming the wonderful change from Chicago, I really had to stop and ask myself why something like this happened when this part of our journey was supposed to be magical. People and situations show up in our lives for a reason. While that reason may not be apparent in the beginning, I have learned to trust that all will work out in the end. Although I never imagined that my boyfriend would eventually die from cancer, I realize that this experience spearheaded my journey of faith. Sometimes this is difficult and I really have to take a step back and wonder why something happened as it did. Even when walking through the emotional pain that leaves you feeling drained and wanting to curl up and not wake up for days, I have learned that this too shall pass. The experience happened in my life for a reason and it is my job to listen and learn and walk this path in faith. In my most difficult days when I question the journey I am on or something pops up that leaves me shaken and wondering why, I immediately head to the ocean and center myself and listen intently to what God and the Universe are calling me to do. I center myself and listen to my body, mind and spirit and let go the need to have to know every single step in advance and completely understand and intellectualize my journey. I walk the path in faith.

CREATING YOUR V-I-S-I-O-N

The V-I-S-I-O-N system that I use in Pathway to Mind and Spirit, Inc. is something I continually use daily in my own life. Although we may understand our greater vision or big picture, small steps are made each day to grow and live into that vision. Each step along the way gives us the opportunity to visualize the possibilities at hand. Visualizing each step gives us the chance to experience the impact it will make. We can then shift our way of being in the world to support our journey by increasing the support around us, owning our path as a true expression of our vision and nurturing it to live into the next level for our lives. Creating your vision is ongoing work on you; it is not easy and takes constant dedication.

V – Visualize

I – Impact

S – Shift

I – Increase

O – Own

N – Nurture

VISUALIZE YOUR FUTURE

For many years I refused to really embrace the possibilities for my future because I felt I was limited by my skills and education even though I had a college degree from a top university, was finishing my M.B.A. and had decided to pursue a Masters in Social Work. I never felt I was good enough. One day I was asked a simple question which started to unleash the possibilities. If you had money to do anything you wanted to do, what would it be? At first I was too closed off to consider the possibilities but when I started playing with it and discovering the gifts that I had, I really started to embrace a new path.

I *visualized* the possibilities for my future. Nature and photography continue to be very important, as are traveling to meet new people and experiencing different cultures, which allow me to understand the world in a more compassionate way. Much of this I have been able to incorporate into my vision for my life and purpose. I write about what we can learn from nature. I re-center myself through nature in an ongoing way. My business is connected to the world at this point through the World Wide Web where I have a following from different cultures and ethnicities. I have met many people through the use of social media and learned that we are connected to the same vision which is to realize a greater future for the world. We are called to leave the world a better place than when we first were born. I am committed to that idea and it is what drives me every day. When I create a new aspect of my vision, I immediately *visualize* the experience and key into how it makes me feel. If I sense any discord then it's not the direction to go because it has to resonate with my intuition which again is Divine Guidance.

When you *visualize* your future, what does it look like? What does it feel like? Many don't understand what a vision is in life or how a vision can benefit one's life. When you tap into what excites you, brings you passion and gives you energy, you will start the path to following your calling and purpose.

IMPACT YOUR LIFE

I realized early on that I am the one who can make the greatest *impact* on my life. Although I realized this, it still scared me to death; the thought of encountering all those emotions daily was not fun. I spent a lifetime numbing the emotions and living in that so-so place where life was just ok. As a child, as I dreamed of the possibilities, my dreams were not supported or encouraged therefore coercing me into an existence I didn't fully embrace. While it wasn't horrible, it also didn't hold any real passion and excitement. Taking the risk has become more important than living in fear. I alone could embrace the emotions and the ups and downs to live into my greatness. I co-create the life I want to live knowing that I can impact the world in a positive way. When I really embraced this way of life instead of living as a victim where nothing was ever right, I knew I was destined to make a difference in the world. I love the emotional ups and downs because it means I am growing, expanding and embracing a new level of life.

What *impacts* your life? Do you embrace that you alone are able to make the final impact on your life. How will your vision impact the world? How does the passion and excitement that you experience around visualizing your future impact your life? What other emotions exist and how do they impact each moment? What are your strengths that allow you to move forward towards your future? What are the limiting beliefs?

SHIFT YOUR WAY OF BEING IN THE WORLD

When I really embraced my vision, I had to *shift* the way of being in the world. I am a spiritual being living in a sometimes mundane world. I intentionally create practices that support me as a spiritual being. The more open and conscious I am, the more I sense and pick up the energy of a situation or a person. I no longer interact with certain people in the same way. I have actively increased the amount of positive people who are in my life and limited the negative ones. Creating a mindset where I recognize my limiting beliefs and sabotaging tendencies, allows me to create practices to help *shift* my mindset and be in the world in a different way. I no longer get up, race out the door to work, run through the day and go to sleep. I intentionally create time for me in the morning and evening to center and connect to my passion and power. I have to feel and embrace the path I am walking. The longer I walk this path, the more in tune I am with my energy and the more I know when I am feeling out of sync with it. When I experience this, I work to realign and embrace the power of just "being" instead of constantly "doing."

What do you do to *shift* your way of being in the world. What limiting beliefs and sabotaging tendencies do you have? What practices do you have that help shift your mindset and be in the world a different way?

INCREASE CARE FOR YOU

I find that I have *increased* the care for me as I am walking this path. I easily spend at least 10-15 hours per week caring for me through meditation, walks on the beach, reading, writing, self-development workshops, affirmations, energy work and building relationships. Part of my requirements for my master's degree is an internship in hospice. While I find the dying process very spiritual and sacred because it is the soul departing from the body it has borrowed, I also experience the physical, mental, emotional and spiritual pain of the dying person and the pain of the family and friends. Times exist when I walk out the door at the end of the day completely drained and I know I must intentionally spend more time

staying centered and grounded; I must have my energies in alignment to feel balanced, peaceful and in tune with the divine connection to the world, so I do whatever it takes to get to that point.

What do you do to *increase* the support for you? What do you
do to support yourself and live a healthier lifestyle that supports
your goals and allows you to live into your best future? What nour-
ishes your mind, body and spirit?

OWN YOUR LIFE

After my boyfriend and father died within eight months of
each other, I was finishing my M.B.A. and decided to do a second
graduate degree in Social Work. Knowing that I had to start working
full-time, I took the easy road and went back to my former full-time
job. My intuition screamed 'NO' but I did it anyway. While I felt
stuck in the job that I really didn't love, I did learn how to create
new aspects that allowed me to have a certain level of contentment
until the day when I knew I had to get out. When you start feeling
trapped and bargain with yourself that you only have to get through
one more season then you know it is time to leave. I *own* the decision I made, and now know and embrace my intuition when other
decisions arise; I listen to and act on my intuition. While I may talk
it over with a close friend or business associate, I rarely deviate from
what my intuition is telling me to do. I *own* my life and can co-create
what I want to have in it. I alone have the final say on what to accept
and not accept. When I make that final decision, I am at peace with
it; I don't feel the angst and over thinking that I used to experience.
I don't question my choices but really embrace my intuition and
know that I am walking my path. My vision is my own and only I can
truly go after it in a big way. Even when our intuition kicks in and
shows up sometimes we still refuse to see it. We alone must *OWN*
our vision and embrace it 100%.

How do you recognize, embrace and *own* that this is your life? Do you create the life you love? Do you embrace and own all the emotions in your life knowing that this helps you continually move forward and take your life to the next level?

NURTURE YOU AND YOUR VISION

Nurturing your vision is about constant care for the growth and development of it. This is a continual process that requires commitment and dedication to you and your work around your vision. I used to think that I would finish school, get a degree and arrive at my dream job; I would have no more work to do other than to walk into this job each day and do it. This was how I thought I defined success. No! *Nurturing* our vision is a moment to moment gift we give ourselves to support our life. It allows us to embrace the passion and excitement so we can face head on the fears and frustrations and say enough!

How do you *nurture* your vision by having practices and people that support you? What do you do to connect to the emotions of passion and excitement so the fears and disbeliefs become secondary to living your life of greatness?

RECOGNIZING WHEN YOUR LIFE IS OUT OF ALIGNMENT

Walking this path has been a blessing in many ways and it has clearly shown me when I am not living consciously. I immediately sense when my life is out of alignment because I feel a discrepancy in my body, mind and spirit. When one part of my energy is shifted out of alignment, it throws my entire being off. For example, I spoke of picking up another's negative energy which I experience through intense emotional strain coupled with the feelings of sadness and pain; I know that when I have the experience, I have to release this energy immediately. It is draining and literally sucks the life out of me. I walk on the beach and embrace the goodness of the Creator and know that more is right in the world than wrong in the world. Recognizing when my life is out of alignment requires me to be vigilant and take responsibility for my self-care. It requires me to set priorities in my life and one of those number one priorities is me!

Our body is an energy system. The seven chakras known by the colors of the rainbow are energy filters within the human body that create vitality and balance in our lives. They include the root, sacral, solar plexus, heart, throat, third eye and crown chakras. When something within our energy system is off, our being is out of alignment and when we are in tune with our spiritual self, we can sense that. When in balance the system works in harmony and creates a life that is well-adjusted and experiences a sense of peace. When out of alignment, life feels off and unmanageable. Habits that support the mind, body and spirit may need to be adjusted. For example, if I ignore my intuition and go against my third eye chakra, then the result is that I continue to intellectualize, ignore the feelings and Divine Guidance around a decision and eventually feel stuck in a life that lacks imagination and possibilities. If I trust in the balance between my intellectual capabilities and intuition then I am able to tap into and nurture my third eye chakra. I am increasingly able to tap into what feels out of alignment in my world and immediately focus on realigning that with my core passions, beliefs and health. The energy or lack of energy directly affects the body, mind and spirit. When in alignment, I recognize that I nourish my body, mind and spirit by making choices for healthy food, positive thoughts and spiritual practices that support me.

IN CLOSING

Every moment of every day is precious and we are called to live into our greatness by discovering and embracing our purpose for our lives. Each of us came to the Earth with potential and we have the choice to accept and live into our gifts or live a life of fear and regret. As spiritual beings, we are continually called to embrace God in every person we meet. We are called to live a life listening to our Divine Guidance and trusting in our journey. I have intentionally chosen to create a life that gives back to the world with the goal of leaving the world a better place than when I came. The legacy I choose to live embraces my gifts and strengths which continue to help me overcome my limiting beliefs and fears. I own my destiny. I challenge you to walk your path of purpose and live into your highest potential. Will you embrace it and live into your greatness?

Namaste

SUSAN MILLER has been interested in health and wellness since early childhood. Her own challenges with illness and stress prompted her interest in holistic health and the spiritual path.

Susan is an accomplished healer and teacher, combining her knowledge of traditional healthcare with energy medicine. As a Registered Nurse, she understands how emotional stress can affect the physical body and likewise how physical stress can affect the emotional body. She also studied Quantum Physics and Energy Medicine extensively, allowing her to work on all aspects of the person: the physical, emotional, mental and spiritual levels.

Susan uses the Indigo Biofeedback device to detect stress on the physical or emotional level and retrain the body in more appropriate ways of dealing with the stress. This helps the client reverse the effects of that stress and/or prevent further stress damage. She also uses Hands-On Energy Healing techniques to detect and clear the energy field of negative stress patterns while charging and rebalancing the field. Susan helps clients understand why they repeat certain negative patterns or hold self-limiting beliefs utilizing The Systemic Family Constellation Approach. She helps the client trace the origin of these negative patterns and reframe the beliefs with clarity.

As a Health and Wellness Coach, she helps clients set realistic goals and choose appropriate action steps to reach those goals. Adding EFT and PSYCH-KTM into the coaching sessions helps the clients overcome the negative self-talk that was preventing them from reaching those goals.

By uncovering the self-limiting beliefs, rewriting the negative patterns and reducing or eliminating stress, her clients experience a more fulfilled and joyful life.

DEDICATION:

I dedicate this chapter to the many teachers in my life that helped me understand and interpret life's lessons, and taught me to surrender and put down my sword so I am no longer ready to defend and go to battle. Thank you to those who taught me to respond rather than react, who encouraged me to step out of my comfort zone and accept growth, and who told me over and over that I AM good enough until I believed it. For those who held the lessons, and those who held the interpretations of those lessons so I could learn how to accept and love all of my life, I am grateful.

Chapter Five

Awakening to Your Truth
by Susan Miller

F.E.A.R.—**F**alse **E**vidences **A**ppearing **R**eal.

I used to be consumed by lots of fears. Ruled by my fears. Most of my decisions were fear-based responses to choices I faced every day.

I have been on a healing and spiritual path for many years now. It was a long time goal for me to follow my passions and dreams, to live in joy and harmony. How hard could that be? But in the beginning of my conscious journey I found that as I took a step forward I got hit with obstacles that created fear or doubt, and I'd take one or two steps backwards into the security of my comfort zone. I know now that it was actually my own fears that created those obstacles, not vice versa. My thoughts created my reality and my results always validated my limiting beliefs.

I grew up feeling inadequate: not good enough or pretty enough; I was too shy, too sad and too dependent. I felt unlovable, or maybe it felt like love came with conditions. This led to very low self-esteem as an adult, and a limiting belief of not deserving more.

So I did this "dance" with myself. I had ideas and moved toward fulfilling those ideas but then thought or faced the "fact" (real or imagined because of fear) that it just wasn't going to work, I wasn't good enough to continue, and I feared facing the shame or "I told you so" if I failed. Putting my goals aside, I accepted that I just wasn't good enough to reach them.

Having completed a number of very deep and powerful trans-formational studies since then, including the 4-year program at the Barbara Brennan School of Healing, the Systemic Family Constel-lation Approach, and several Shamanic healing sessions, I can now understand why I had certain fears. It took shifting my core beliefs through those studies to change the deeply held negative patterns that stood in my way and made it difficult to do what I wanted to do. My passions remained a dream, my purpose never quite within reach, and my personal, professional, and business goals were never quite fulfilled, until I learned how to trust, surrender, and allow the shift...in spite of the fear.

THE BACKGROUND

Growing up, I was taught that it was selfish to ask for anything. I was told to appreciate what I had because life is about working hard and not expecting or asking for anything more. I was told to believe and to do as I was told; that to question was defiant and rude.

It seemed selfish to want to be happy. The limiting belief I internalized during my childhood because of feeling inadequate was, "I'm never going to be good enough to have more." So I learned to give up on my goals and dreams; they were to remain my fantasies. No good would come from searching for happiness or a deeper meaning for my existence. This was my "lot in life." Accept it and live it.

My childhood experiences motivated my marriage to an abuser; my husband reinforced my limiting beliefs, adding layers of negative self-talk. I was told outright that I didn't deserve things because I would never amount to anything. I was punished for asking for things, doing anything without asking for permission or making any decisions on my own.

When my children were young, their dad refused to continue supporting us, even though we were still married and living together. I returned to work earlier than planned, to afford school supplies, clothing, and winter coats for my children, birthday presents for their classmates or ice cream from the neighborhood ice cream truck. Before returning to work, I was repeatedly told in front of the children how worthless I was. After returning to work, I was repeatedly told in front of the children how incompetent I was for leaving them and how I didn't love them. On numerous occasions he called me at work to tell me he harmed the children because I left. I would race home and find them crying because he didn't allow them to play, talk, or have any fun. This usually ended up being *my fault*. I was just wrong, no matter which decision I made. For those first few years I started and stopped working many times, trying to make the right decisions to make him happy. I tried to choose the best ways to make my children happy but that seemed to backfire.

If you're thinking, why didn't I leave or get help... I tried! The first year of our marriage we lived with my mother and step-father while we built our first house. One month into the marriage my husband hit me and dislocated my jaw. Before going to the hospital, I told him to pack and leave. But when I got home from the hospital I found him crying, and he manipulated his way back into my family's mind once more.

So this was my lot in life. Just accept it and live it.

I felt like I was watching a suspenseful movie where I had to keep asking, "Who is the good guy? Who is the bad guy? What's happening here?" But this wasn't a movie. I didn't comprehend the plot in my own life; things didn't make sense. Life seemed too painful and wasn't producing many joyful results. I seemed to be living Murphy's Law, and I couldn't understand how things got so messed up when I was always on guard, trying so hard to be good and to do right. I merely existed; I wasn't living, or at least not living with purpose and passion. I was an empty shell wanting more from life but not really believing there could be more.

From my experiences, I believed I would never be good enough, pretty enough, or successful enough. Happiness didn't seem to be an option. But I wasn't content feeling like a failure at relationships, family, career choices, and friendships. My existence revolved around my failures. The focus of my daily life included challenges, mistakes, fear and the ever-present negative attitude of "what next?" And that negativity was fueled by the words I heard or the messages I interpreted from people in my life that I trusted: I was just not good enough to deserve more.

Throughout my life I gave away my power. I allowed myself to be held back and held down from allowing my own spirit and vision to soar, from following my passions and living my dreams. I didn't know I had a choice. I saw no safe options. However, deep down I didn't want to accept this as my lot in life. I knew I had to silently keep searching for that spark of joy and not give up hope that it was indeed possible to find it.

Surely life was not meant to be a negative experience. I wanted a life where my children knew I loved them and was doing all I could to make them feel safe and secure in their world, not as fearful as I felt. But it seemed I perpetuated that pattern of fear or worse, a pattern of anger and hate.

And I was the easy target. For years, the children were told by their father that I didn't love them, that I was wrong about everything, that they had every right to be defiant towards me, and I was not "in charge" of the home so they didn't have to listen to me. And they complied.

I blamed a lot of people for my unhappiness. It took me many years to learn how to look inward for the answers. Once I was able to do that, it took many more years to learn how to let go of the self-blame, self-loathing and guilt in order to trust my own 'inner Voice' to find joy and live with purpose. I had to learn how to follow my own dreams and passions, not what other people expected of me or told me to do, and not what I thought I should do to please anyone else or to be good. I had to learn how to have the courage to follow that guidance, and let go of the fear.

BEGINNING THE JOURNEY

Much got in the way of living my own life. I felt as if I were on a roller coaster, one with lots of twists and turns that was supposed to remain on the preset and predetermined track. Yet my roller coaster was veering off track at every turn, changing the course of my intended life. My reality snuck up on me by surprise. Suddenly, I was not living the life I had dreamed of or planned.

I always envisioned having a loving family where each person felt safe and respected, free to express ideas and where we could sing, dance, and play games without retribution. But in my reality, my family didn't feel safe and loving. For example, when driving I had to keep the children quiet so their dad could listen to his talk radio. We were not allowed to talk, listen to or sing nursery rhymes or play games. And after his long day at work, he demanded the same. The children had to be fed and ready for bed so he could relax; I had to keep them quiet and out of his way.

Intentions.

Many of the events in my life were shaped by my intentions, but I certainly didn't end up where I intended. What are intentions? Are they just wishes? Dreams? Some dreams are like nightmares. How can you change the course of your life intentionally then? How can you get back on track if you have been so far off the intended track for so long? I spent much of my life asking how to do that, and getting the wrong directions. Or maybe I didn't know how to listen to the directions well enough, or I was listening to the wrong people and not my inner guidance. Maybe there were too many hurdles or obstacles that I didn't know how to navigate. And certainly there was a level of not trusting in the directions I was receiving.

Intentions are important, but we must first change the beliefs that keep us stuck in the negative. What we think about and feel, we continue to manifest; so the more we maintain fear and doubt, the more we attract more fear and doubt. I wanted to learn how to align with my intentions, not with my fears.

Goals.

Goal-setting: Writing intentions down on paper and taking action steps is so imperative. It's important to look ahead and not dwell on the past. The past is full of regrets, guilt, mistakes and pain. When we dwell on past challenges we didn't overcome or focus on the change we didn't make happen, we stay stuck in our "lack" mentality. So we must find a way to accept and resolve the past in order to move forward. Letting go of the blame, the judgments and regrets seems so simple, yet it's complicated to let go of those attachments. Our story was built on those limiting beliefs, and who are we without our story? A better question to ask is, "who are we meant to become, in spite of our story? Creating goals give us the plan to become what we intend.

Trust.

It seemed when I trusted, I got hurt. I thought I had dealt with this challenge but it kept repeating. Learning to trust our inner guidance system, *in spite of the fear*, is a step towards transforming the limiting beliefs. The universe sends us lessons in the form of challenges until we learn to trust. Put another way, what we think and feel we manifest more of. So if we feel gullible or inadequate, we bring more situations into our lives to validate that. The universe will send more and more challenges until we do learn. Trusting our 'Inner Voice' allows us to learn more quickly.

Purpose.

I searched for a very long time to determine my purpose. First I had to believe that there was a purpose to my early experiences. I had come such a long way, yet I was so far from what I wanted or thought I *should* be doing with my life. It was time to get out of my own way, get past the fear, do what I wanted to do, and step out of the safety of the comfort zone.

My safety zone was the *known* terror and torment of my marriage, as strange as that sounds. *The unknown* was the possible result of my intentions to leave, which were usually met with threats to harm me, and worse, to harm the children.

For years I chose my *known* life, as hard and painful as it was. But my comfort zone didn't feel safe anymore; it felt limiting, frustrating and constricting. I had settled for the "less than" life and I was suffocating.

I knew my purpose involved helping others heal; now I had to align my goals and dreams with my intentions and emotions. If I was going to make a change, I had to begin thinking and feeling differently about my experiences, changing my attitude and beliefs and learning to replace fear and anger with love.

Attitude.

Attitude can make or break a day, a relationship, a job. It seems easy enough to keep up the good attitude, but how can someone maintain a good attitude while always trying to balance, from moment to moment, which decision is the least damaging? How can one feel consistently positive when every day decisions are fear-based, full of mistakes or regret, or unfulfilling outcomes?

I regretted most of my life's decisions, and worse, I was blaming myself *and others* for having made so many mistakes that now seemed to be so far out of my control. Every decision I made was undermined; the children were told for years I *was worthless*, and they began acting accordingly. I was now living my nightmare and couldn't wake up. My attitude was based only on my failures and lack; I was consumed with negativity and depression, and I nearly lost hope of ever finding any joy.

But it's that attitude that will keep you stuck, and it's that attitude that must be shifted in order to create change. Finding comfort in a support group for people in difficult relationships, I felt validated and began to learn about choices I didn't believe I had.

Choice.

It's a choice to move forward and be happy, to *live* life and not just exist. I existed for most of my life without that deep sense of peace and joy. But which choice is better, or right? Is it really selfish to ask for one's needs to be met? Every action requires a choice. So how do we choose between being "in the flow," and being proactive, between allowing shift and controlling change, or between trusting the universe and holding onto our story of who we are? To me, being proactive means taking action to *make* something happen, and that necessitates expending physical, mental, emotional or spiritual energy. And expending energy is not the same as allowing effortless flow. Sometimes it feels too "hard" to be proactive, to move towards a goal or to make a dream a reality. And are we then "in the flow" of allowing? So how do we balance the need to be proactive with effortless intention? One choice at a time, one step at a time - the flow will happen once we choose to start the process.

Balance.

I felt so out of balance wishing for more than I ever thought possible; I experienced so much fear and so little joy. To stay in my marriage, I needed to find the balance that gave me a sense of self-worth and a safe outlet. That balance was my work. I was really good at my job and I loved working.

I was brought up with the "work hard" mentality: *You're not supposed to enjoy work; you're just supposed to work hard.* I began to bury myself in my work. The more I stayed out of the house, the more disconnected I became from the pain; but I was also disconnected from love. I had finally gotten good at something...numbing myself.

I finally realized how *messed* up that work hard mentality really is. I believe we are supposed to enjoy work, live with passion and purpose, and love life. We can take action and not have it be hard work. We can work long hours and enjoy those hours and the results we get from them. My struggle was twofold: the letting in and allowing change (fear-based thoughts about the potential punishments) and also in the asking (risking vulnerability). I was afraid to really ask for what I wanted. Maybe it was the "do I really deserve this?" mindset I had internalized.

Taking action doesn't have to feel "hard," but can it really be "easy" to manifest? Maybe the answer lies in the difference between "hard" and "frustrating." And maybe the frustration came from my being impatient.

Patience.

I had a lot of resistance to waiting; patience was not one of my strong traits. Wondering *if* something will happen and when it will happen. I felt non-productive. Waiting seemed to spark my super-ego and the negative self-talk to run rampant, thinking I wasn't receiving because I didn't deserve. Or it would trigger my superego to tell me that I was being lazy, a familiar dialog. Keeping busy kept the negative thoughts distracted better...or at least buried better.

Processing.

Processing is exploring the deeply held feelings and core beliefs, busting the myths and uncovering the truth, and realizing that the limiting beliefs were based on filters that no longer serve us. We layer new emotions on top of the original wound, the initial pain, with each trigger. Processing is amazing when you get the Ah-Ha's. It's about looking within to find the answers, not looking at the other person in blame and judgment. It's about stepping back, looking at a situation with a new perspective, and examining our role in the situation. We can then shift our awareness to come from a higher place, not from the ego. It's about changing that old pattern of reacting which keeps us stuck in the victim mentality preventing us from growing, and choosing the most appropriate way of responding.

Processing is ultimately a good feeling, but it's critical to actually go through the pain of remembering the initial wounding leading to the limiting beliefs, and understanding the child consciousness leading to the current triggers that remind us of that initial wounding. Why is it a trigger for me? What does this remind me of? What lesson can I learn from this?

It's important to go through process sessions with a professional and to follow up regularly as the new images and beliefs take hold. Through these sessions, you allow yourself to acknowledge and feel the pain then let it go. Of course, it's easier to stay numb, to forget or give up, but that perpetuates the story. There's a freeing in feeling the emotions and releasing them, like weights being lifted, and we gain understanding and clarity. Reliving the pain is worth it, when you really "get it" on the deeper level, the spiritual level.

THE PHYSICAL JOURNEY

My journey into the holistic healing path began with my own health crisis. I was feeling stuck, unable to move forward in spite of desperately wanting to. I was sick and getting sicker. Stress had wreaked havoc on my body and my emotions and I didn't see any clear way out.

I came to realize that it was my fear of the ramifications, the punishments, of moving out of my comfort zone that manifested the excuses I needed to remain stuck. I couldn't allow myself to grow; I didn't give myself permission to grow and I needed to accept that to remain safe. And that false sense of safety came with a huge price, namely my health.

After going from doctor to doctor and receiving diagnosis after diagnosis, I was giving up hope of ever moving forward and finding joy. But it seems the universe had other plans for me. I was fortunate to have a good friend introduce me to holistic healing.

During the last year of my marriage I was diagnosed with several illnesses, most of them induced by or exacerbated by the stress. It began with daily migraines accompanied by bright flashes of light coming at me, which had me rolling on the floor in agony feeling like my head was being squeezed in a vice. At the same, time I was suffering other neurological symptoms. My memory had been declining. It often became a game for my children, having them guess how to get us home. I was losing strength, falling down, and getting lost in the small hospital where I had worked for eight years. I was diagnosed with Lyme disease and began a regimen of strong antibiotics, but soon I worsened beyond belief. The antibiotics exacerbated the once dormant Epstein Barr Virus, and systemic Candidiasis along with Fibromyalgia and Chronic Fatigue overtook my body. I was bedbound, unable to function. My blood pressure was uncontrolled, alopecia developed, and I gained 40 pounds in just a few short weeks from my metabolism nearly shutting down. I couldn't eat much due to the GI symptoms and side effects. The sicker I became, the more my ex-husband told me and the children I was worthless.

By starting on many nutritionals, herbal remedies, homeopathics, energy sessions and a strict juicing diet, I gradually improved. The physical healing was accompanied by emotional support, finding out I did have choices and beginning to shift my core beliefs, thanks to the support group I had become so attached to. After recovering, I sought to learn more about how I could share this amazing journey with others who likewise saw no clear way out.

I was transforming. And for the first time in years I appreciated life. I was able to find the guidance and support that I needed to show me that there was a way out. Trust, love, and ALLOW-Shift! set the pace for that journey.

THE *SPIRITUAL* JOURNEY

Some people call the spiritual journey the *Awakening*. I believe it's an awakening to one's truth, one's soul's journey; it's as if we have been asleep, dreaming, and just now bringing this information into our conscious awareness. Allowing ourselves to accept change and growth, we allow the dream and the longing to become our new reality. We step onto our true path by surrendering, trusting our inner guidance, and letting love flow.

It definitely is a shift not only in the conscious thought process, but also in the deeply held core belief system that holds the key to our growth and development spiritually. I had to learn that I do deserve happiness and I deserve to pursue my passions. Then I had to learn *how* to do this.

I knew my fears of leaving my marriage were valid and could potentially lead to harm for me or my children. But my fear of being harmed also existed in my marriage. My challenge was how to leave the marriage with integrity and faith while preserving our lives.

Can you recall a situation where you felt uncomfortable? What about your first day of a new school when you were a child? Some may experience this as exciting, and some might remember a feeling of fear and anxiety. That's because some people are better prepared for growth and look forward to the excitement of growth, while some of us believe early on that fear is inevitable, or that we seem to have no control over our life. Regardless of which feelings are elicited in you, I know you can understand how frightening it might be under certain situations to move forward. It may have been scary for you to leave your parent but leaving your parent behind meant moving forward. Have you gotten married, or gone away to college? Leaving the home of your family of origin was necessary in order to move forward in life. Pushing ourselves to the edge of our boundary, or even past that edge to the other side, is the only way to really grow. The process is similar to the way a butterfly needs to grow out of its cocoon by pushing through the edge of its boundary. And each time we venture out, we push that edge further back and expand our comfort zone. This is how our soul grows.

Once I learned that it was okay to search, to look for happiness, to let go of the negativity, the fears and the *shoulds*, replacing them with optimism and hope, my world changed forever. But I had to be reminded frequently that this was okay and not a bad thing; I had to be reassured that searching was movement forward and not defiance. I had to be coached, trained and taught that I was actually entitled to live a life in joy and with purpose. And it's not only an entitlement, but it's my birthright, *OUR birthright* . . . to live in joy and with purpose.

I had to learn to trust in the process of surrender and accept the guilt of growth. Since I had been in defense and on guard for so long, I had to lay down my sword, surrender and let love flow. I had stopped the flow of love for so long by numbing myself to all feelings. And moving forward towards something new meant leaving something familiar behind, causing guilt. I was stepping out of my comfort zone. Growing pains can hurt and cause fear, causing many to retreat back into safety, or they can bring a smile to our face when we realize that leaving comfort is how we grow.

Being in a long-term abusive relationship, I had a very low self-image. Since I had been punished for asking, questioning, doubting, and trying to stand in my own power, I had too few and inadequate skills for how to pursue my life with purpose. It led me to make choices that caused lots of messes, some of which I'm still cleaning up.

But they are *my* messes, not fear-based decisions; they are not *his* choice for me or her choice for me, or the choice from my superego, that nagging voice telling me I wasn't good enough. They were my own choices; I was finally learning to stand in my own power, to choose how to live my life.

My attitude from the new challenges I faced transformed from the "what now or what next" negativity into a newfound appreciation for life's lessons, and an optimistic and enthusiastic joy for what else would make me feel great and feed my soul. I felt alive! I was awakening from my "merely existing" life to living and feeling joy.

Challenges that we encounter are just like hurdles on a runners' track. To the runners, hurdles don't represent roadblocks or challenges they will not overcome, but rather momentary obstacles that can and will be maneuvered in order to continue on the path. Similarly, we must acknowledge and learn to maneuver our own obstacles in order to get to the finish line. As we learn how to jump over each hurdle, we learn the lessons that move us further along our spiritual path.

It's important to do what you love and love what you do. We were not put here to be miserable, to exist while waiting to die. We were given free will for a reason: to make choices. Choose happiness! Create your reality. Feel your emotions because they give you the guidance and information you need, and they are the catalyst for manifesting. To feel is the way forward; to feel and to trust those feelings steer your soul's growth.

I now risk discomfort and trust my inner guidance system; I hold onto my power, and I feel love and joy. Able to open my heart where it was closed for so long, I am now able to forgive.

Forgiveness.

Forgiveness is a critical part of your soul's learning process. In order to truly surrender and move forward, we must learn to accept our past, acknowledge our part in the events as they were, and forgive. We cannot bury the past or hold any resentment. We cannot hold blame or judgment. Those emotions keep us stuck in the victim mentality and the story. We can only move forward when we rewrite our story from a place of understanding, acceptance, and love.

But true forgiveness is not about forgiving the other person, as most of us believe. It's about understanding *their* filters - where the other person is coming from; it's about understanding *your* triggers and reactions, and forgiving yourself for allowing your power to be given away in your reactions. Accepting the lessons these emotions taught you, you take responsibility for your part in the incident or event and let it go without punishing yourself.

Through my training at the Barbara Brennan School of Healing and with the Systemic Family Constellations Approach, I learned how to forgive myself for stepping into an abusive marriage. I learned what my soul needed to stop the destructive pattern. I learned to put down my sword, surrender and stop the battle. I uncovered the roots of my limiting beliefs that set the stage for my low self-worth, and set them free...with love. Without these lessons of forgiveness, I would not be the healer that I am today.

Listening.

It's not easy to initially listen to your 'inner Voice'. It can feel too risky to think about fulfilling a dream, and seem like an unsafe choice. It can feel like abandoning your true self. But in reality, listening to your guidance reaches into your core to *awaken your true self*.

By pushing through my fears, I stepped into my power and found passion and purpose in my life. Through energy work, I now assist my clients in looking inward, tracing the negative patterns and limiting beliefs that cause stressful situations to repeat in their lives, so they can begin to see a new truth. Clients gain insights and clarity, so they can let go of the story and clear unresolved issues. Energy work can affect physical, emotional and mental stress. I facilitate the journey of self-discovery as I assist my clients on the path of growth. We work together to create a life of joy, happiness, and optimal health and wellness.

YOUR AWAKENING: TRUSTING YOUR INNER GUIDANCE

Whose voice have you listened to that was critical of you and your efforts? Who told you that you couldn't succeed at something, or you shouldn't try? Who told you that you weren't good enough? Whose voice have you internalized that has now become your inner critic?

The inner critic is the superego: the voice that tries to keep us in the status quo, the voice of a critical parent or another authority figure, which we still listen to as if we're still the child. This voice wants to keep us safe in our comfort zone. But safety comes with the price of not moving forward, and this keeps us from fulfilling our passion and purpose.

The 'inner Voice' that wants you to succeed is the voice we are meant to listen to; it's your guidance system. That's the positive voice, not the critical voice; the one that whispers suggestions based on love, not fear, but it takes patience to trust, to listen, and to choose the voice of love, growth, and guidance.

It takes challenging your belief system and readjusting the filters that you see through to be able to accept and trust the process of growth. Don't be afraid to dream big and set big goals. The goal isn't big enough if it doesn't bring up some *fear*! Those butterflies in your stomach represent your soul getting ready to jump the hurdles and buckling up for the ride! The butterflies want to fly beyond the safe boundary. If the goal isn't big enough to bring up some fear, it isn't big enough to shift your inner guidance to make a change.

When planning to move forward and choosing the action steps to follow your plan, don't become attached to the outcome. Attaching to the specific outcome locks you into a box and doesn't allow for the universe to deliver results in another way. See it as you want it to be, feel the emotion of *already having met that goal*, and then let it go. Surrender and allow it to unfold as it's meant to unfold, without the need to control how that happens.

And be *patient*. If you stay focused on the feeling of "I can't wait to have that," you remain in the emotion of *not yet having*. And you don't want to continue to manifest the *not yet having*.

If the true desire is to choose safety, that's perfectly okay. Only you can choose your soul's path. As long as it isn't connected to you giving up your longing, repressing your feelings, or regretting this decision, then it's the correct choice for you. If, however, you still have a spark of that "what if" feeling, if you're giving up that choice out of fear or the superego lecture, then perhaps it's time to look to that other 'inner Voice' and follow your guidance. Choose from love.

Susan Miller 561-445-4878
www.BalancedWellness.net

DR. CHRISTINE CHICO, a former anesthesiologist who now specializes in the health and wellness holistic industry, helps people live a healthy, soul-fulfilling life.

With a background in health and wellness science, and as a practicing medical professional, Christine is passionate about working with clients who want to have a focus-forward approach to healthy living. Through her various medical positions and experience, she discovered that the body has an innate potential to heal itself and is devoted to bringing this message to people around the world. Christine has long known that when people feel healthy, they feel powerful, and she works with her clients to help them understand and maximize, the transformation that occurs when the soul, body and mind are in alignment.

Christine knows from experience what can occur when someone is "successful" in life but not really happy. Her work in metaphysical healing allows her to guide others to look within and harness their inner strength, both physically and spiritually, so they are able to create a life that is in balance and brings them joy.

Christine's clients say she is caring and knowledgeable, and has an intuitive ability to diagnose what may be wrong very quickly. They also say she is compassionate while still bringing an element of fun to the alignment process of healing.

Having functioned as the Medical Director of a well-known health facility, Christine is currently enrolled at the Sedona University of Science as a Doctoral candidate. She is the author of numerous publications, including an article featured in the Journal of Medical Society of New Jersey. Christine is developing her new line of products and programs that integrate health, wellness, anti-aging, weight management and spirituality. She is looking forward to the launch of these in 2012.

DEDICATION

I dedicate this chapter to my daughter, Marita. She is my light: in dark times, when I may have thought of giving up, my love for her gave me the strength to move forward. Thank you Marita, for the joy you give me as I watch you grow into an incredible women. Being your mother is the most rewarding part of my life.

Chapter Six

Finding the Gift in You
by Dr. Christine Chico

What is your definition of success and prosperity? Do you look at success in terms of establishing yourself at the top of your field and prosperity as earning a large income? I don't believe my definition was very different from most. I once thought of prosperity only in terms of finances and success in terms of accomplishment that would cause others to take notice. But God showed me some difficult lessons before I realized my thinking was wrong and I became a receptive student. It took years for me to discover why I chose my path and examine if it was truly the right path for me. Multiple setbacks happened but failures are the only way to know success, so I continued on. One Friday evening in May 2009, I received a phone call that was a bigger blow than I could have ever imagined; God got my attention and I had to do some hard soul searching which is what this story is about.

PROSPERITY

To my own surprise, and to most people who knew me growing up, I became *successful*. I completed a level of education I had never imagined, and was rewarded very well financially. I accomplished things I never thought possible. I identified goals and focused on them with passion. It was a rough road but I managed to achieve the goals I set. I received a degree in Osteopathic Medicine and became Board Certified in Anesthesiology. Once I began my own medical practice I earned an income I never dreamed of achieving. I worked long hard hours to reach that level of income and at the time the money was my driving force. My husband also had a position for which he was paid well. The combination of our two incomes provided an incredible lifestyle.

Life seemed good. I spoiled myself and family; however I was able to live below my means and put money aside without making any sacrifices. We were in Las Vegas and compared to where I came from and most peoples standards, I was living the "High Life." I lived in a beautiful home, ate at fine restaurants, frequently used a limo service or helicopter to get around town, had box or front row seats for events and experienced dream vacations.

At 4000 square feet, my home was smaller than those of most people I knew. Well-known people lived close by and it was exciting to know that I was living so close to celebrities and the celebrity lifestyle. Within a mile of my home lived a number of sport stars and well known entertainers. I was close to Wayne Newton's home and would stop at his fence to watch his horses in the front yard of his ranch. Gladys Knight, Robert Goulet, Michael Chang, Mike Tyson, and David Cassidy all had homes a very short distance from mine. On one occasion President Bill Clinton spent the weekend at my neighbor's, security was all over, and for that night our block was a spectacle. Although his arrival was televised, I watched the crowds from the balcony off my bedroom. His departure was less of an event; I was able to chat with a Secret Service Agent while waiting for his limo and see him up close when he was not expecting an audience. A well-known actress once lived in my house, before I owned it, while she was in a production of Sugar Babies on the strip. While I embraced this life, it was upsetting to me that my daughter referred to a typical middle class neighborhood as the ghetto; needless to say our neighborhood was a far cry from the inner city where I grew up.

My lifestyle at this time was also very different from what I had known in the past. I had full-time assistance, frequently live-in help, with my daughter and the house. Most of the household work was delegated to someone. My ex-husband could not be expected to do household repairs. With my level of ownership for household duties who was I to judge?

I did take care of the groceries and cooking when we had home cooked meals. At times we ordered in; Las Vegas had a wonderful service that delivered from many different restaurants. Home delivery was brought to a higher level. The delivery man was dressed in a tuxedo and served the food at our table, which was far from the delivery we had growing up; all I can remember was having a milk man! We frequented many restaurants, at times enjoying a private dining room. It is not unusual to receive preferential treatment when you have more money; what is odd, the more money we had, the more we were comped.

Las Vegas has a wide range of entertainment and I enjoyed much of what it had to offer. On multiple occasions, we were the guests of the performers. Working in the golf industry, my husband went on the golf course with entertainers, and I met people involved in entertainment while practicing medicine. On multiple occasions we were guests of performers we had met who gave us complimentary admission and preferred seating. I had the opportunity to be the guest of local headliners, classic rock stars and magicians. When we did pay for admission we always had great seats. We either bought them or the right tip usually got us the seat we wanted.

We had a boat on Lake Mead - at first, a 23-foot "cuddly cabin" but it did not take long to find that unsuitable. We found a 32-foot cabin cruiser. When I had a night that I wasn't on call, we spent the night anchored in a cove. The next step was a 52-foot sailboat; we did not keep that on the lake. When we bought the boat it was located in Ft. Lauderdale so we would fly to Florida and sail to the Bahamas for a few days. Later the boat was moved to Tortola BVI and four weeks of the year we sailed around the British Virgin Islands.

It seemed I had the lifestyle made from a dream. As my practice became more established I made more money and had greater control of my schedule. While that should have made me happy, I was not happy. I experienced bouts of depression and dissatisfaction with my work as well as increasing fatigue and a variety of physical ailments. I cried without reason and experienced frequent headaches and GI problems. I had difficulty concentrating and maintaining focus. I couldn't find the energy to get out of bed and withdrew from most activities. After seeing multiple doctors and several courses of medication there was no improvement. I was no longer able to practice anesthesia. I began to examine how and why I got to this place and where I was going from here.

UNDERSTANDING THE PAST TO EMBRACE THE FUTURE

I was born and raised in Camden, New Jersey. Not long ago an article in the Wall Street Journal gave Camden the title of the poorest city in the United States. In the 1950's it was not too bad, still not what is called a middle class neighborhood. It was an area of mixed ethnicity, mostly made up of Italian, Puerto Rican and African American. Comments my mother made led me to believe we were one of the poor families in the area. My mother referred to other families as rich because they had fathers; my father passed away when I was two. I was taught that prosperity was achieved by having a man around, but we did not have one and my mom did not seem to be interested in remarrying. I now understand why I was married and divorced three times; to be successful I needed to have a husband.

My mother had a limited education, completing eighth grade; she left school when her father died to help support her mother. When she worked it was always in some sort of factory. During World War II she polished windshields for fighter planes. What I do remember was her working in a dress factory. She was paid on production, fractions of a penny for a seam. She worked part-time and several months out of the year. We lived primarily on Social Security benefits, which limited the amount of money she could earn. If she earned too much she would lose her benefits. I did not get the impression she was interested in earning more and was comfortable with what she had.

My mother was one of nine children so we always had family around. Several of her family members lived with us in a three bedroom house where I shared a bedroom with my mother and brother. Our home was filled beyond capacity.

Mom loved to cook and entertain. She saw life as one big party. One of her sayings that I remember was "Whoever doesn't like this life is crazy." In addition to family, we always had friends around; it was a very interesting group of people. The people my aunts and uncles invited were Italian with very interesting nicknames. My mother never missed an opportunity to have a party. Everyone came through the door with either a case of beer or a jug of wine which was always consumed. Even my birthdays were celebrated this way and not with other kids and a cake.

My mother wasn't mean or cruel, but I did not feel that she was really interested in being a mother. She was a widow at age thirty with two small children, two years and six months of age. After my father died, it seemed that for the first time she was able to make her own choices and it was all about her. She did and still tells me she loves me but I never felt it came from the heart. Her past is still a mystery to me; she is very secretive about it.

She kept a roof over our heads and food on the table. After that, my brother and I experienced little else materially and emotionally; she spent little time with us. I don't ever remember being tucked in or being read to at night. We were usually sent to bed at 7pm, on our own. She slept in and I fixed my own breakfast before I was old enough to attend school. I remember in first grade being told to have my mother cut my sandwiches in half; the teachers didn't know I made the sandwich. On another occasion, I woke her to ask her what color the light needed to be before I could cross the street.

My hygiene was questionable and my clothing limited. On one occasion she sent me to have my hair cut, but the barber sent me home because my hair was too tangled to put a comb through. One snowy morning I needed to walk to school and I had no boots. I was able to improvise foot covering for myself by taking plastic bags, putting them on my feet and using rubber bands around my ankles to secure them. This managed to keep my feet somewhat dry. I went to Catholic school so I wore uniforms but periods of time existed when I had no other clothing but the uniforms. After school I was forced to stay indoors because I did not have a change of clothes. As one might imagine, I was seen as different and teased by the other kids.

The hardest part of growing up was my mother's ignorance to the psychological abuse inflicted on me and my brother by her brothers and sister. Many times I would go to her crying and she would respond "they're only teasing." I was called fat, clumsy, and lazy by family members. On one occasion, my aunt broke my doll because it was funny to see me cry. My mother even used what she seemed to think were terms of endearment toward me that were very derogatory; they were Italian phrases, one referred to a part of my anatomy and the other to a profession I was much too young to engage in. Later in life when I questioned her about the words she used, her response was, "I didn't mean anything by that."

The female role models during my early development were not women you might expect to direct me to a professional career. My mother had four sisters; the oldest died before I was born; two married at age 14. One never worked outside of her home, and the other was divorced after 25 years of marriage, at age 39. She worked full-time at a dress factory, which today would most likely be called a sweat shop. The fourth of my mother's sisters never married. While living with us for several years, working in a variety of factory jobs, she eventually found a male friend, unavailable for marriage, but able help her with her own apartment.

Growing up, I felt I was different. I had many times when I felt I was not in the right place because I did not feel I was with the right people. As a child I cried, "I want to go home," never having any idea where home was. I knew I did not want to be like the women I knew growing up. I had no idea about who I was, where I wanted to go, or how to get there. To top it off, I did not believe I could do anything nor had opportunities to make any changes.

As I became an adolescent, I experienced many of the same issues, although some things changed. We moved to a suburban neighborhood, where I had problems fitting in. My mother remarried; he was much younger than her and they lived together for a while before they married. Because of this I had difficulty maintaining any friendships. Some parents were not accepting of my mother's boyfriend and would not allow their children to associate with me.

We were in a nicer home and neighborhood but still poor and high school is all about fitting in. At this point I was in public school because we could not afford Catholic high school. Gone were the uniforms which had helped me fit in. I remember kids calling out, asking if my dress knew its way to school because I wore the same one regularly. I had no interest in attending school and frequently cut class. When I did attend I did not participate in class work. My grades were marginal which resulted in my being moved to more remedial classes. Becoming increasingly shy, introverted and insecure, I wanted to drop out, get a job or attend a vocational program.

I looked for any type of work because I knew if I were to have anything of my own I had to earn it. Although I was too young for a real job, I found work as a mother's helper and after a while as a baby sitter. This helped and I was able to buy a few articles of clothing for myself. The first thing I bought was a pair of pants from John's Bargain Store, unfortunately not the height of fashion, but I had something to wear after school. When I was 15, my father's sister called me with a job opportunity. She was a nurse at a local hospital and they were looking for weekend help. I jumped at the opportunity.

I began working as a nurse's aide. I went to work every Saturday and Sunday at the hospital from 7:00am to 3:30pm. Since the only bus that got me there was at 6:00am, every weekend I was at the bus stop at five minutes to six and arrived at work a half hour early. The work was hard and required a lot of responsibility especially for my age. Although I was not very happy with the job, I now had spending money. I could buy "stuff" for myself, and that was all that mattered at the time.

Since I was working in nursing, a career in nursing seemed like a good idea. Although I was not happy with the work, I thought if I advanced in the profession it would be more enjoyable. To be eligible to attend nursing school meant I had to change my school habits, take appropriate classes, and make good grades. I enrolled in the necessary classes, despite protests of the guidance counselor who insisted the work was beyond my ability. I began to study biology, chemistry, and advanced math and I loved it. I found the study of life fascinating and enjoyed the challenges of the classes. My grades improved and I was able to gain admission to nursing school. My mother seemed pleased and I was thrilled to have her approval. One of the selling points of nursing school compared to a college education was the nominal cost. I was able to get tuition, books, uniforms, room and meals for a few hundred dollars per year; college cost a few thousand.

The first year of nursing school went well. I enjoyed studying the life sciences, Anatomy, Physiology and Chemistry and Microbiology. Although very little study of nursing occurred during this first year, we had a few hours of lecture on topics related to nursing and a few hours in the hospital each week. During summer semester, we had one full day of lecture on nursing topics and four days of hospital experience. I hated it! I realized my real interest was how and why human beings worked and not nursing. I announced to my family that I intended to leave nursing school to attend college to study Biology. My family's response should not have come as a surprise because no reason existed to spend money on me to go to college. I had a younger brother and if any money was to be budgeted for college it would be for him. The money would be wasted on me because he would have a family to support someday and I would not. Nursing would be a nice job for me, something I could always fall back on after I raised my family.

I dropped out of nursing school ignoring the protests of my mother and began looking for a job. What I found was nursing was the only skill I had and began working as a nurse's aide once again. Then I made the decision to return to nursing school; if I was

103

working in nursing I might as well become a professional nurse. At this time my mother felt she had given me my one chance so when I returned to nursing school it became my financial responsibility. I took out loans and returned to nursing school hating every minute. I did not find the studies very challenging and put very little effort into them, basically just enough to pass. I did take classes at a nearby university at night to fulfill my desire for more academic studies.

When I received my R.N., finding a job was easy but I was not happy with the work. I did accomplish one thing; I made my mother happy, something I did not feel I had done in the past. My mother's approval always seemed important, but I found it really did not make me happy. I continued to work at various jobs hoping to find one I enjoyed but that never happened. So I went to college part-time to pursue a degree in Biology with the intent of heading to graduate school. My studies went well and I received good grades. My advisor had taught at a dental school and frequently told of the horrors of graduate programs and the advantages of having a professional degree. He encouraged me to look at Dentistry but after some investigation I found it did not appeal to me so I looked at other options and applied to an Osteopathic Medical School. I was accepted at a New Jersey state school and enrolled. I believed this would make my mother proud and also show the rest of my family that I was very capable; I also proved my worth to the high school teachers and guidance counselors.

I made it through and continued to become a Board Certified Anesthesiologist. After 20 years and much financial success I had to give up my profession due to health reasons. I was not troubled by this because I lost passion for my work. I had my finances in order and that seemed to be all that mattered but that security did not last for long. Several bad investment decisions took away all

I had worked for. I still had my degree and license so was able to support myself, but I went through several jobs and never found the right fit.

THE GIFT REALIZED

The final blow came. I became entangled in a legal issue that is literally threatening my freedom as I write. God finally got my attention. One Friday evening in May 2009, I received a phone call that caused the most drastic change in my life I could ever imagine. I was informed that I was facing charges that could result in spending the rest of my life in prison. I can't detail the circumstances that led to this call, but I can say the issue was a total surprise to me and it was not related to a time when I was earning large sums of money. This call got my attention. I have never been so surprised or afraid in my life. That was the moment that forced me to take a step back and have a long hard look at me. I realized this is not a dress rehearsal and there are no do-overs.

I experienced three bad marriages, dealt with the death of my father, stepfather, grandparents, three close cousins, 10 aunts and uncles, and a daughter. My life went on. From the experience of my childhood, my primary motivations were to prove my worth to others, to obtain approval and to seek out financial rewards. Today, most of the people I sought approval from are gone and so is the money I earned. My very freedom is being threatened. *All that is left is me.* Now I have to ask me what is it that brings me joy, what do I really want? Did I make choices for myself or someone else?

I think back on my desire to study life science and wonder if it answered the questions I was really asking. As I went into more and more detail there were more and more questions, which were never *truly answered.* I learned about the human body in terms of organs, which are made of cells, organelles, and composed of molecules. All molecules are made of atoms which can be broken down to sub-atomic particles. How does all this stuff work and stay organized? Physical science did not have the answers I was looking for. I began to study Quantum Physics and Metaphysics in hopes of finding answers and I came to realize when it comes down to it, only one answer exists. The intelligent force in the universe, God, is holding it all together. Having now begun my spiritual studies, I am finding more answers. I have learned that to get the right answer you must first ask the right questions. I forgot the first question in the Baltimore Catechism that I memorized at the age of six, "Who made me?" and the answer "God made me." I am learning I need to live my life for God and myself, no one else.

Are you living your life for you? Are you really doing what you want in life? What situations in your life influenced your major decisions? Looking back, I realize most of my accomplishments were done for the wrong reason. Once I found a way to improve myself and my life, I proceeded with fierce determination, but I did it to prove that I could succeed to others. I developed a "look at me now" attitude and not a true sense of fulfillment. When I reached a goal, people still told me I was crazy. When my mother spoke of my accomplishments, they were hers. She talked of how expensive school was and how difficult it was for her. The approval I sought never appeared. I worked so hard and was still so unhappy.

How often do women try to make other people happy? We frequently live our lives for others, looking for approval. Do you find it hard to say, "No?" Are you concerned about what others think when making decisions? Are you frequently looking for compliments? How often do you ask questions? "How does this look on me? Does this make my butt look big? Did you like…?" I took it to an extreme, but I think we are all guilty of the same behavior to some degree.

When I don't look for approval and get it, it means so much more to me. Recently, when out with my boyfriend, I did not ask my usual question, "Do you like the way this looks on me?" I got dressed and off we went. We went out for several hours and when we got home, he commented, "I really like that outfit; it looks great on you." This compliment meant so much more.

Would your life be different if you lived it for you? While I don't recommend ignoring others' feelings, being unconcerned about how decisions or behaviors affect another or acting in a way that would harm someone, I do suggest focusing on what makes you happy. Do what feels good to you! You want to take the afternoon off and read a book rather than fixing dinner? Do it! I never heard of a family dying from a meal of soup and sandwiches or pizza. Heck let them eat cereal! Pick out something you want to wear, look at yourself in the mirror, give yourself approval and do not ask another soul's approval! Look in your heart every morning and plan to do what feels good for you. When mommy is happy the entire household will be happy.

I took the need for approval to an extreme. Although it would be easy to blame my need for approval on my childhood, the "speed bumps" taught several lessons. Besides learning I need to live my life for me, I have also learned to take responsibility for my life. When I attempt to blame others for my situation, I become the victim. Only by taking full responsibility for my life am I truly in control. Your actions and your choices are the only things that make your life what it is. It is not the actions of others that determine who you are and how you feel. When you take full responsibility for the actions and decisions you make then and only then are you living your life.

The need for financial success was also a big influence in my life. I thought having "stuff" would bring me happiness. I will not lie and say I did not enjoy the things money could buy but I can say I was not truly content. To spend my day watching the clock, wondering when I could go home and counting the days from one vacation to the next was not the sign of living my life with purpose. Most of the time, I did not even realize that it was possible to do something you loved and earn a living. Work was meant to be difficult and unpleasant. Play was when you had fun and enjoyed yourself. I never imagined that people actually were able to pay their bills doing something they enjoyed. As I continue to open myself to new ways of looking at life I see new possibilities. Spending time with happy content women has been an inspirational awakening for me. I still have doubts about my purpose and how to accomplish it but have identified the problem and am ready to seek the solution.

Can you imagine being in complete control of your life? What if you decide how each day will be and how you will feel? Imagine earning a living doing what you love and enjoy. Is this how you currently see your life or do you need to make some changes? What do you need to do differently to accomplish this? The first step is to identify the problem or where change is needed in your life. Then take baby steps to make the needed changes. You don't have to make a total overhaul at once to begin to move forward.

I simply started by putting a smile on my face every morning before getting out of bed. When I do, then the first thing I see when I pass the bathroom mirror is a happy, beautiful woman and that feels great. It is me. I end my day reviewing what I am grateful for. To keep that from being a repetitive exercise I put letters in a cookie jar. Every day I pick a letter and throughout the day I identify things that begin with that letter for which I am grateful. I make a list of at least five items and review it at the end of the day. These two small exercises changed my life.

I found it important to change the people I spend time with. On one occasion, when I heard Nancy Matthews, the co-founder of

Women's Prosperity Network, speak, she said if you want something behave as if you already have it. She went on to explain it was not a matter of pretending. It is simply identifying with someone who already achieved what it is you desire, observing those behaviors, and behaving as they do. I now seek people who have positive outlooks and are satisfied with what they are doing in life. They remain positive, believe in a Higher Power, trust their intuition and continue to move forward looking at any setbacks as learning opportunities.

I started reading self-improvement materials and meditating daily which has resulted in changes in how I approach life. I have learned to maintain a positive mental attitude which has changed my life. I have no control over tomorrow, I cannot change yesterday but do learn from the past. Having recognized that I only have full control over today, I find the importance of living in the moment; I am not living for what I might obtain tomorrow because I am grateful and enjoying what is here and now. Set every moment with the intention you want. The thoughts we think become our reality, so make them good thoughts.

We are all at our core vibrational energy and our mental mood influences the frequency of our vibrations. We then attract similar vibrations to us. Feeling good is a high frequency vibration and will attract more of the same type of vibration. Bad feelings set up a lower vibrational energy and will attract more of the same. Many physics studies show different vibration frequencies attracting similar frequencies. In medicine the relationship between mental attitude and health and disease has been observed. Now researchers have been able to measure hormonal and neuro-chemical changes in the body change with changes in mood. The beneficial hormones and chemicals are at higher levels with positive emotions and feelings. The ones that can cause damage to the body have more negative feels and emotions. Thoughts do become things. Researchers have also demonstrated that an "attitude of gratitude" has been linked to better health, sounder sleep, less anxiety and depression, higher satisfaction with life and better relationships with others including romantic partners. When you are grateful, you receive more for which to be grateful.

I am grateful for every breath I take and see each one as a miracle. While I won't go on about every detail that goes into breathing, I could. It makes my head spin to think about it and I have made enough people crazy when I speak about the miracle of life. I am blessed to be living in paradise. I have fairly good health, a roof over my head and wonderful people in my life. When I look at the big picture, I am happy where I am and with what I have. When I look back, there are many things I would rather not have experienced but all life's experiences have made me who I am. They have gotten me to where I am today. To some it might be hard to believe, but I am happy and grateful here and now.

I can truly say I have always been a spiritual person and believed in God. I was not interested in organized religion and made little effort to keep God in my life. I viewed God as separate from me. In May 2009 I had to take a hard look at what is really important. I began reading a variety of authors' writings on spirituality and practicing meditation; I realized God is the center of all things. Being the Type A personality I am hesitant to admit I am, I looked for more and more information. I came across the Sedona University of Metaphysics and thought if I am going to do all this research it would be a good idea to pursue a degree. I am now enrolled in their Doctoral Program. My studies have opened a whole new world for me and a new way of thinking. I do not truly know what I will eventually do when I receive my degree. I do know when I was using Google to search for reading materials it was not by accident that Sedona University's site ranked high on my search results. There are no coincidences in life. I am happy with the life I have, although I would have preferred a different path but I know God has a plan for me. If one thing in my past were changed, I would not be where I am today. I realize people may want to take away my tomorrow, but I will not let them steal my today. Regardless of others' intentions, I can control my now, my feelings and goals. Would you like to live your life this way? With the power of God and "the Voice" inside you, life is yours to control. Follow YOUR vision!

CARLA VAN WALSUM PHD, LSHC is a Relationship Expert with a thriving holistic psychotherapy practice in South Florida. She has helped hundreds of clients make quantum progress through her unique combination of psychological, spiritual and metaphysical approaches.

Her extensive study of European, American and Eastern philosophies provide the foundation for her work. These clinically validated techniques and powerful alternative approaches have helped many clients to heal acute and life-long patterns of emotional pain, struggling relationships, family burdens and stress.

Carla's style incorporates a great sense of compassion, intuition and empowerment. Each client is treated with respect, in an environment that is nonjudgmental. Clients include individuals, couples and children struggling with feelings of depression, anxiety, addiction, adoption, divorce, effects of wars (Holocaust, Vietnam etc.), lack of life purpose and other challenges. Carla works with energetic principles to elevate consciousness and awareness of a client's true potential to create the best possible future.

Carla's career began in her native Holland, where she studied Psychology and Integrative Psychotherapy. She is a Systemic Family Constellations facilitator having studied directly under the direction of Dr. Bert Hellinger.

After moving to the United States with her family in 2004, she pursued her vision of bridging traditional and metaphysical approaches by delving into a doctoral program in Trans-personal Counseling.

Carla speaks 6 languages and in addition to her personal counseling work, is a published author, a popular speaker and workshop presenter.

Certifications and training include: Systemic Family Constellations; Non-violent Communication; NLP; Neuro-Emotional Integration; The Work; and Hypnotherapy.

She is the creator of Happy Children, Happy Home™, Life's Hidden Truths™, Peace around Divorce™ and Peace around Adoption™.

www.CarlaVanWalsum.com www.LifesHiddenTruths.com

DEDICATION

This chapter is dedicated to my beloved sister Ineke (Dinah) 6-28-2011.

Being at the extreme end of autism, she never spoke a word. Her total emotional isolation and her inadequacy to enjoy what was offered to her, was embedded in a deep despair of being worthy of love. She was my teacher in compassion. May the angels guide her to the highest regions of light and peace, where she will be able to embrace love fully.

Chapter Seven

Life's Hidden Truths:

The heart remembers what the mind forgets. About love, trauma, metaphysics and Systemic Family Healing

by Carla Van Walsum, PhD

MY PERSONAL JOURNEY

It took crossing an ocean, leaving my friends, family and career behind and losing a lot after we arrived in Florida, to truly follow my inner voice. To actively learn to TRUST, when all else falls apart and to allow my mind access to that humble deep place of knowing, that all is well.

I LET GO of fear and practiced BLESSING everyone and everything as the Essene Jews did 2000 years ago; this practice replaces many hours of therapeutic counseling work. The energy around you clears and shifts totally, and helps free you from any negative attachment and circumstance. I placed myself on the path of being

GRATEFUL for what was, although I left the Netherlands where I had a wonderful life and everything was easy, to help me survive.

Why did we leave our home? My children became increasingly afraid of being Jewish in a growing Islamic presence in Rotterdam. The 'not again' thought made us decide to move. Simultaneously deep down I knew I needed to spread my wings and Florida would give me that opportunity.

Two phrases often whispered in my head: "LOVE is the answer" and "COMPASSION is needed." The whispers, which identified themselves as coming from Archangel Uriel, started when I was a kid. Yes, I am listening, Universe, show me what to do! Love is certainly the most powerful of the energies that the Universe provided us to use as our free choice for wellbeing. Yes, we simply can choose love, to let go of fear which is so destructive. The Life's Hidden Truths work shows how love's flow is often entangled in families.

WWII, which caused 60 million deaths, impacted my family enormously. Growing up I felt the urge to contribute to a more compassionate, peaceful world. How? I didn't know. Psychology seemed to be the answer. Psychology impassioned me, but I had studied music and had a successful career as a concert flutist; I wasn't satisfied. I went back to college and studied Psychology & Integrative Psychotherapy and I arrived at my true passion. As I was becoming a mom of three lovely kids, I slowly developed my practice.

While still in Europe I sought additional healing resources for my clients, more than clinical psychology and psychotherapy offered. I noticed that talking about the past and about what is wrong or missing, brings you back to the misery and often leaves you stuck. What you focus on expands. I wanted my clients to emotionally heal and be happy! Thus, I searched and studied alternative, clinically proven modalities. I was totally blown away by experiencing the greatness and effectiveness of Hellinger's Systemic Family Work which often provided almost instantaneous emotional and physical healing! The discovery of the presence in our family heritage of our 'emotional genes' that unconsciously influence so much in our present lives gave rapid insights and clarity for people and businesses. Systemic Family healing became a big part of my work, a great tool for many obstacles.

Arriving in the U.S. in 2004 with my three young kids and husband, I set the intention to meet only wonderful people and I did! I wanted to create my path and be of service to others. But it was a lonely journey as well.

My intention was to help raise consciousness and open people's hearts to love, gratitude, blessing, forgiveness, respect and compassion while creating an environment where non-labeling and non-judgment would be a driving force. I blended my holistic practice with Integrative Psychotherapy, Psychology, Metaphysics, Systemic Family Work (Constellations), Hypnotherapy, Non-violent (Crystal Clear) Communication, NLP, Abraham Hicks, and Transpersonal Counseling which I studied in the USA. Intuitively I knew that Florida is meant to become a center of LIGHT.

LIFE'S HIDDEN TRUTHS: INSIGHTS IN FAMILY AND PERSONAL DYNAMICS.

We all have a story. We are born into a family and part of a family soul. Family souls contain collected data of the past generations of people, places and events that affect our lives today—our *Hidden Truths*. Life's Hidden Truths™ (Systemic Family Work) are a unique method of awakening our knowledge of our inherited family dynamics, personal dynamics and emotional patterns and how dynamics relate in *individuals, family, work and life*. Through unconscious loyalty and love to our family system, we can unknowingly become identified or merged with previous family members, often repeating their destructive patterns and manifesting similar afflictions and unresolved issues. This legacy can have a tremendous effect on our lives as well as our children's live. Once these behavioral genetics, our epigenetics, are brought to "light," a profound and deep healing process begins, giving way for a life changing journey of personal discovery and growth. In this chapter are examples of how this work can change perceptions and physical wellbeing.

Some reflections on Family, Relationships & Divorce

My true vision is a world where people love themselves and feel loved in their families, with respectful communication and time and compassion for each other. They are healed and released from emotional baggage. After clearing the sub- and unconscious blocks, they are ready to manifest their true selves, purpose and dreams. They have a perfect connection and balance with intellect and intuition.

My vision inspired me to design parenting classes: Happy Children, Happy Home™, relationships and personal growth workshops, and Life's Hidden Truths™ to awaken in others their brightest self. When our baggage is released and our mindsets reprogrammed we are able to own our lives and destiny.

Life becomes a wonderful place if every obstacle in life is seen as an opportunity for growth instead of taking a pill to numb/suppress the symptoms or to cover the cause. When we come from the perspective of using positive words and language, then the 'opportunity for growth and learning' is empowering; we become disempowered when we use the labels 'disorder, disease or illness.' These labels keep you stuck. If you HAVE it, you won't lose it. Our sub- and unconsciousness takes our thoughts and statements for granted. It is impossible to set and manifest clear goals for health, wellbeing or success, while the pressure of the past is distorting the process.

This book is published in 2012, which is predicted to be the end of the world. But which world, the world where ego, force, punishment, and FEAR dominate? It would be great if that world disappeared... When fear is involved, love freezes. It would be awesome to live in a fearless-loving world. Each of us has the choice to choose between the dichotomy of love or fear.

Yes, *love* is the answer. Love is the master healer. I once read about the mystical Rabbi, the Ba'al Shem Tov (Poland 1700's), who recommended to parents when they came for guidance about their children, "LOVE THEM MORE". This statement resonated and filled me with tremendous joy! I used it immediately in my family counseling practice. It freaked the parents out!!! Because we are raised to try to control, individuals in the family, behavior at schools, through hierarchy in the workplace, many don't know that control does not really work. Control is fear-based; why not raise your child with TRUST? 'Loving your child more,' when he or she behaves in a way you don't like, appears ridiculous to many. But is that really true? Are your child's decisions purely wrong and negative? Control is often very judgmental. Who likes to be judged all the time? A child who hears a parent say "I don't trust them," will certainly not feel the urge to show how trustworthy he is. It's a lost cause already. It is shocking to me to see how easily children get grounded because of lower grades in school or perceived wrong doing for just being themselves? What do we create? Anger and resentment. Punishment is often revenge, a low energy, unnatural consequence, not the law of cause and effect. If my son borrows my car and causes an accident because he drives too fast, the consequence is he can't borrow my car. That is not revengeful punishment but honoring my own needs. As parents and teachers, we often bring our own frustrations; controlling ourselves is already difficult enough. We can ask respectfully for compliance and expect the best.

TRUST is a concept that disappeared out of the western general consciousness; it is the opposite of scientific thinking. When we watch or listen to the media, trust disappears and appears irrational. The brain, a divine creation, exists as a tool for smart decision making. We need to trust logic as well, although, it is here where metaphysical insights become interesting. If I send out trust energetically to someone or something, that positive energy is felt by others and influences situations for the better. Trust, as well as kindness, respect and goodness need to be practiced, and we have to receive it before we can give it.

In my work as therapist, I observe that the *absence of love* is the main problem behind almost everything. So, the healing answer would be: to add and reinstate love. Words, the tangible manifestation of thoughts, are a great instrument to do that. Say kind words to you. Look in a mirror three times a day and tell yourself, how lovable you are! Can YOU do that? This works as 'self-hypnosis' which is nothing more then re-imprinting facts that you will believe one day, like you did with all the other things you heard. Of course you need to DELETE the unwanted beliefs about self. If YOU don't love yourself, how can someone else love you? How can you love others, if you don't feel loved? What you don't have you cannot give! If you want to attract a great mate in your life, be sure that you totally, unconditionally feel loved and appreciated by you! If you don't love yourself, you will find someone who will resonate with that doubt.

The unconscious and subconscious minds and part of our soul contain the data of all of our experiences. If words are that powerful, then we need to choose them wisely. It was quite shocking to learn about research done in the U.S. showing that an average 16-year old heard that he was not OK 180,000 times. Why do we have the right to criticize others? Education does not equal criticism. As children we are supposed to take seriously all the comments adults say about us. When we are adults, we buy self-help books, run to a therapist or take a pill to make us *authentic* again. As adults we learn, "**Do not take it personally!**" It is someone else's perception; reputation is nothing else then others' opinions. So, why would you care about reputation? If a child replies to a teacher or parent in this way, I am not sure that wisdom would be appreciated. At first we are raised to behave a certain way or we get punished; later, we need to restore our authentic self, and learn that opinions don't matter that much.

Your opinion isn't better than another; it's only different. Being right or wrong is just not that important because that's the ego speaking. Relationships improve tremendously when people learn this.

What really helps to improve communication is to observe *without* evaluation, criticism, analysis and judgment. When you see and observe you stay with the PURE facts, not your opinion. Evaluation is the judgment of someone else, and judgment NEVER stems from love. For example, "You are lazy" becomes "I see you are lying on your bed, would you please clean up because *I need and value* a peaceful, harmonious home." So, in this way you connect with YOUR needs and take responsibility instead of blaming another for not meeting your needs. This is one of the powerful ingredients of Crystal Clear (Non-violent) Communication.

To be raised in a culture that works with the rule *Do this and you'll get that* won't create and stimulate independent free thinkers, only people who are attached to the outcome. It is great to do something and to get nothing. You do for the joy of doing; that's authentic. You live for the joy of living; that's authentic too. Joy is taken away if every step is measured. Aren't we supposed to experience a joyful life?

LOVE is the most important energy to make life worth living and to create the highest good. Babies who get fed but experience no love simply die. What about all those kids who just get enough love to stay alive?

In our intimate relationships we mirror and encounter our deepest issues and our unresolved relationships with our parents. Want to be happy in your relationships? Then create peace in your heart with your parents. No matter how terrible your childhood was, your parents were also a product of their circumstances. While not excusing them, YOU learn to grow in compassion for yourself and for your parents. Hold in your mind and heart the picture, "You gave me life, and that was the greatest gift you could give me. I can take care of the rest." This is a typical part of the process and sentence from the Systemic Family Work.

If you experience a lot of pain, work needs to be done to heal and let go. It's a simple decision and powerful step to direct your request to any guide or higher power of your choice and say, "I let go of my pain! PLEASE heal my heart." It is here where spirituality and metaphysics in its free form can provide healing. If you continue to sit on the victim chair blaming others and circumstances, then you will continue to give your power away. A victim attitude blocks all healing. Acknowledge the pain, heal and let it go.

How many couples do you know that radiate great love for each other after many years of togetherness? It is bliss that divorce is possible, not a curse. It is a CHOICE we can allow if nothing else helps to make it work. When we hear that people are married for 60 years, we congratulate them. Why? For surviving and persisting in a situation that for some was wonderful, for some was maintained out of fear of being alone, for some was hell, or for some it was simply IMPOSSIBLE to make a different choice.

Structures and philosophies of the past pushed us to marry young, fast and preferably for a lifetime. The guidelines given: don't spend too much time trying, looking and experimenting. Many believe that the marital commitment solves the feelings of 'loneliness.' No, it does not. You first need to fill that hole before you commit.

We need enough time to find a suitable partner. Since many don't do that, living a happy fulfilling life might include divorce, but everything can still be great. It's not the divorce that is the problem; it's how the couple handles their anger, disappointment, pain and fear. It requires humbleness to acknowledge each other's pain, disappointments and weaknesses, the entanglement of one's own life drama. Blame, guilt, and shame are the strategies people use. I am so hurt by you that I will hurt you back so you can feel how terrible I feel. Forget about that. Why not authentically show the other how we REALLY feel? That is most difficult, because for ages feelings haven't been acknowledged and honored. Almost everyone knows the statement: 'Only I am responsible for my own happiness.' But hardly anyone knows HOW to do that! One of the great parts of the Systemic Family Work is that the deepest entanglements can effortlessly be resolved. The core of the issue gets right in your face.

It is very helpful to change the observation you make and to learn Crystal Clear Communication in order to look through a compassionate heart-based filter. "He is cheating on me" might become, "My partner is looking elsewhere to find love because he is not able to allow himself the love that I offer."

"She's having an affair" could be changed to, "They have a miraculous connection." The ways we tend to look at these themes is VERY judgmental and usually causes much pain by the involved people. Why such blame and condemnation? Almost everyone experiences the deep hidden fear of abandonment. The Systemic Family work shows that we seem to have a deep longing for finally having the perfect mother - that strong symbiosis of unlimited nurturing and unconditional love. When we are in love, we touch a part of that perfect world. Our desire for criticism, for being right, and our incapability to enjoy simply what is destroys that state of bliss. One reason most of us LOVE chocolate, is because cacao contains phenyl ethylamine (PEA), which is also released by the brain when we're in love. The bliss chemical, Anandamide, is found in cacao as well and is released when we're feeling happy. Lift your vibes: eat more (good) chocolate!

A divorce can be an opportunity for learning for the children as well. When everything is calmed down, the possibility arises for new relationships for the parents with others. That means a new opportunity to show the children a love-filled, well-functioning relationship. Love heals. Never ever replace a parent. I went through a difficult divorce (is it ever an easy process?) and my kids never had a low grade in school. To focus on the good parts in the other person can be of much help. The energy between people aligns when they are producing the same kind of positive (or negative) thoughts. Yes, that requires work of the mind and the heart.

Sometimes people say that so many boys coming from single parent homes are in trouble because their moms aren't able to guide them well enough. Aren't the difficulties coming from the deep pain and anger within because they feel totally abandoned and not worthy of love by their father?

The situation prior to a divorce can be a lot of misery. Don't speak about a broken family because who wants to belong to a broken family? You now have two parents who live in different homes. The *Systemic Family Work* offers deep healing for the situation in a divorce. Restoring the respect for the partner restores balance. It requires you to let go of being right and focused on your own vision. Speak the words, "I honor you as the father/mother of our children. Thank you for creating this fantastic family." The power and energy of these words is felt by the whole family as a system. Other members don't need to be present to perceive the benefit.

When a child comes to my practice seemingly with issues as a result of the changed family situation, I ask him to choose from the colored footprints, a tool from the Systemic work. They are in various sizes and colors and each chosen pair will represent the persons involved with the issue of the child. When those footprints are laid out on the floor, the way the prints relate shows the dynamics in the family as perceived by the child. Feelings, thoughts and resources can be chosen and are helpful as well. Where do love, sadness, and anger belong? The children put them intuitively and this often, surprisingly, shows the inner picture of the child. Children love it that no difficult questions are asked or need to be answered.

The parents are often shocked by what they see - the loneliness and the distance their child experiences. "But we do not talk bad about each other," parents often say. Well, they do not need to. Their thoughts, feelings, and energies, are totally taken over by their children.

LIFE'S HIDDEN TRUTHS: SYSTEMIC FAMILY HEALING

Everything is energy. Everybody has an energy field, a kind of organizing field that sends the atoms and molecules of our emotional, mental, spiritual and physical bodies to where they belong. This field contains our consciousness and is perceived through our senses of knowing, feeling, sensing and hearing. Our individual energy field is always connected to the people around us.

The family energy field or the family soul with all the collected data influences every individual of the family. This field is immediately noticeable when we 'set up' a constellation. After brief specific questioning about the issue, the client chooses representatives from the audience. The representatives function as receivers and transmitters of information and then a hidden world unfolds. It is not pschychodrama!

Constellations that involve other issues than family related, such as personal, illness, work, or organizational, are called phenomenological; they go quickly to the heart of the matter.

The well-trained facilitator guides the process from the initial issue to resolution. When solution sentences are right on, everyone in the audience feels the rightness of it. Huge shifts take place in the deep conscious levels of the client's soul as well as others in the constellation.

Divorce

Recently I had a woman, Eva, who had done a lot of therapy, in my workshop. She was concerned about the behavior of her ex-husband, who according to Eva never grew up, had addiction problems, and did not take responsibility as a father. Those were the reasons for divorce. Eva seemed to be very hurt because their children were disappointed by his lack of accountability and she couldn't be both parents in one. When a parent leaves the family, either by abandonment or death, the child cannot digest that with the mind, but it is taken in with the heart. "Because you left me, I am not worthy of love, otherwise you would have stayed." That's the simple way of perceiving the world as a young kid does. Feeling unlovable can become a block hindering successful commitment in intimate relationships. I told Eva that all a child needs is to have happy parents. So if one is falling-out, the other needs to work on being happy and positive, making it light and turning away from the drama. Focus on the good that is ABSOLUTELY still around.

We started the constellation by choosing Eva, her ex and her two kids represented by unknown people in the audience. Hardly any information was given; they were 'blank,' the perfect state to perceive information.

The representatives for the kids showed strong loyalty entanglements, felt unstable and insecure, were moving between mom and dad. In order to bring the parental relationship back into balance, the parents need to acknowledge each other in *total* acceptance.

126

That clears the energy field of the couple relationship and the kids feel lighter. In bowing your head for each other and saying, "I respect you as the father/mother of our children, I let go of all the pain we caused or you caused," it creates a profound feeling for the couple, and works even if the other parent is not present.

We feel and notice the energy from each other all the time, but we are not consciously aware of it. My client couldn't say those words. Instead she said, "Respect needs to be earned, not granted." That contains a judgment and a condemnation. Behind that is the pain of what happened. I answered her that respect can come from the love for that person, from compassionately understanding him. When she held on to her grudges and disappointment and continued to observe him only from her perspective and not heal her pain, Eva's family situation would remain like it is now. The father's representative actually mocked the way Eva controlled him; he felt not seen by her. Criticized. The anger and frustration that he showed was huge. He couldn't look at her, and stared all the time at a spot on the ground, which indicates another perspective.

"Who died in his childhood," I asked Eva.

"His father. He was 14. He loved him dearly."

"Is your ex suicidal?"

"Oh yes... ".

And there is the problem. It is devastating for a child to lose a parent. The pain can be too big. "I miss you so much dear Dad, I will come too." A deep longing for reunion in the soul can lead to the wish to leave too, quite unconsciously. Suicidal thoughts. Addictive (destructive) behavior. Strange illnesses. "It is too scary to love because the pain is too deep when I will lose that person." Children whose parents die young often have an unconscious loyalty to follow down the same path. An intellectual understanding is not enough to shift the behavior.

Eva was shocked with those new insights. What a constellation can accomplish is the healing movement, in this case between (the dead) father and son. The father would say words as given by the facilitator, like: "I love you dearly. I am so sorry. I do love you so much. I want you to live your life fully. Your task is to be a father to your children. You come later." The well-known concept, survivor's guilt, is similar.

Adoption

In Holland, where I was born, a huge idealistic climate in the aftermath of WWII for creating a better world took place. Overflowing from love and great intentions, thousands and thousands of children were brought to the Netherlands for adoption. Good schools, food and love offered them a great future, or at least a better life. After 20 years, research showed that much had gone wrong - 72% of the adopted children showed signs of emotional damage and developed troubled relationships. Talk therapy didn't work well. In the 1990s when the *Systemic Family Constellations* became known in Europe, desperate adoptive parents or their children attended a workshop.

As much love that the new happy parents feel for the child, it is often difficult for the child to take that in. No mindset can help a child through the painful separation process; for the soul, it is a terrible thing to be given away. A baby, no matter what age, KNOWS and feels that. Often it is also terrible for the biological mother and for the adoptive parents who give so much and feel powerless.

Sophia, 22, came to my workshop. Adopted at 10-days old, she grew up in a very loving family with several adopted children. Sophia says she really loves her adoptive mother and gets along with her very well, but she really wants to meet her biological mother which is thwarted by her mom. She wrote her real mother a letter several months ago but received no answer.

"What is the reason you want a constellation," I ask. Sophia works very hard on her personal growth. She thinks there is a connection between her fear to fall in love, shown when she pushes boyfriends away, and the fact that she did not make peace with her mom.

"What do you know about her?"

"She is a crack-whore; she had several children and gave them away."

"You know," I said, "we don't know the story of your mom that made her become who she is now. It most probably isn't a happy one. It will benefit you and your mom if you find words that show her some compassion. I know that every mother deep down somewhere feels pain when she cannot take care of her own children. If she doesn't feel that, life hasn't treated her well. You carry in you your parents. Make that picture soft and warm."

Systemic orders show that the real parents need to be called parent. Adoptive parents better have a different name. Honor your parents in your heart, even if that is difficult. It's one of the 10 commandments... which were I found hard to comprehend in ALL situations. Becoming and being at peace with your parents, whatever has happened, serves you in your life. If you really want to be happy in life and relationships, that part needs to be healed. You know that forgiveness does not condone what happened, but let's go in order to free you.

We set up representatives for Sophia, her birth and adoptive mother. It soon becomes clear that there is not much respect felt by the adoptive mother for the birth mother as shown by the judgment about abandonment and neglect of the infant.

"You made such bad choices!"

"For you a good thing," I said," that's why you have this beautiful daughter!"

Both women looked angry at each other...The birth mother turned away to cry silently and deeply. "I could not take care of my children...Nobody ever took care of me. I am empty."

When energies are calmed down, I let the adoptive mother bow her head a little for the birth mother. "I gave you my daughter, and I thank you for all you gave her that I could not give."

She bows her head in reverence. "Thank you for giving me your child. I couldn't have children myself. I gave her my best." Both women bow to each other; a profound movement is made. Holding respect and honoring what are necessary ingredients for a family.

Sophia is observing her constellation and very moved. I let her step in the field, opposing her two mothers. She bows for them and embraces them, a long, long embrace. A strong energy is felt in the room. Everyone is moved. A movement in the soul is made, forgiveness, acceptance, compassion, honoring each for who she is. Pain of ages is felt. Love flows freely. Sophia sighs when I ask her to take the picture in, a picture of peace beyond our perceptions.

Five days later I call Sophia to check in with her. "Guess what happened?" she said. "My biological mother called me two days after the workshop." Wow, I am so happy for her. Feeling ignored for so long, and suddenly there is contact... That is the power of working with energies by allowing the Soul, and the wisdom of Spirit to work. The simple choice made: Allow GOOD in your life to happen. That is what Systemic Family Healing can create.

Affects of War

War is the father of all problems. War affects the soul in many ways. The innocent boy, who serves his country as a soldier, and throws bombs on a city, is haunted and captured by the souls of the dead. He cannot sleep well anymore; he becomes unwanted, a perpetrator and responsible for the death of many. Energetically spoken, the victim and perpetrator are entangled; the closest relationship that exist. The perpetrator-energy connects with the victim's family and vice versa. One family member can suddenly have totally different behavior then would be expected. Also, if someone loses a large number of family members like in the Holocaust, it has a huge impact on him and the family and can affect even members who never met those dead family members.

The following constellation is a classic example for Jewish Americans. Leaving your country, like the East European immigrants did, was a tremendous step. They collected all the money they had to buy a ticket to the new world. Often one or two children were sent, in the hope that the rest of the family would come later. Those teenagers left everything behind and put their energy into making a living in order to help the rest of the family to come over.

Sara, a 54-year old pharmacist, hopes to get clarity as to why she cannot bond in relationships. During her whole life, she has felt lonely.

"I don't know why", she said. "I have many friends, but I had only one real boyfriend in my life."

"What happened in your family?"

"My parents were born in the US. My mom's parents left Poland when they were 15 and 16. They met on the boat, stayed together and married."

"How is the relationship with you and your mom?"

"Ok, but aloof. Not warm."

We set up the constellation. Sarah puts her mom behind her; the mother keeps her distance from Sarah. She seems not to see her daughter. She is focused on a spot on the floor. Then she walks to that spot and bends over, sits on the floor, very sad.

"What happened to the family left behind?"

"They got killed in the Holocaust - 89 people on her side. Both my grandparents had large families."

The constellation shows that the mother of Sarah is totally connected to the dead. She is tied to the past, not present in her life as a loving free person. Sarah is entangled too and not bonding with the living. Resolution here is difficult and heavy.

Forgiveness cannot be given in the name of someone else. We don't have the right to do that. Reconciliation in this process can occur when the perpetrators feel the pain of the victims, when they mourn together about what happened. The permission the dead give to the living to take their life is very moving. Survivors' guilt often disappears.

Epilogue

I truly hope that Americans will open their minds to the Systemic Family work as has happened in so many other countries. Unthinkable solutions and changes are provided where hardly any equivalent is to be found and it is great to combine with other modalities as I am doing. The focus in the world is shifting towards a more holistic and healthy lifestyle. When people heal from scars of the past, a totally different society will emerge. When we utilize the powers of mind and soul to heal, our heritage will show that cure. Healthy-mind healthy-body is around the corner and the choice for chemical pills could diminish. Since science shows that our DNA can change, we can impact the future of ourselves and generations to come! 2012: Renewal. Change Your Life, Change Your Future!

LAURINA ANDERSON is a Success Coach/Trainer, known as "The Energy Shifter." She is no stranger to challenges. Raised in a basement apartment on the south side of Chicago, this high school dropout, married at eighteen, found herself at the age of twenty-six, a single mother of two lovely daughters (one of whom is mentally disabled.) Struggling to make ends meet, Laurina knew "lack" all too well.

Determined to thrive, she received her Masters in Social Work (MSW) from Aurora University, and subsequently became an Addictions Counselor. Working with addicts served as the foundation for what was to become her life's passion and purpose; transforming peoples' lives for the better.

Laurina made the commitment to become a personal life coach in 2000. She trained under best-selling author and self-help leader, Debbie Ford. Laurina has read countless books and attended all the major spiritual seminars. But it wasn't until her move to Fort Lauderdale that she finally encountered, studied and mastered the techniques that are now enabling her to move her clients forward in quantum leaps.

In her 14 years of business, Laurina's clients come from all walks of life. At age fifty-six, Laurina is just now hitting her stride—growing younger and more energized every day. She states; "I love my chosen career, my clients, my life and the people I'm coming to know as friends."

Laurina knows that "everything is energy" and it is energy that directly impacts your wealth, health and relationships. She is dedicated to helping her clients get present in the moment, quieting the mind, clearing the blocks, shifting their energy into their power and creating their vision.

DEDICATION

I dedicate my chapter to my two beautiful daughters, Lisa and Michele—Lisa, for being my right-hand girl and best friend, and to my Michele, who is my biggest fan. You both have supported and given me the motivation to continue giving all I've got. You have taught me to never stop, love unconditionally, without judgment and from the depths of my heart. Thank you for choosing me as your mother. I am honored.

Chapter Eight

Fully Charged Now
by Laurina Anderson

Well Hi There! Welcome to this part of the book. It's really such an amazing group of authors all within this single place. I know you've been learning so much. Excellent, but watch out, it's now time to take you even further on that upward climb of knowledge, insight, and experience. Yes, you'll get an experience from reading this chapter. But before we go there, I'd just like to acknowledge you. I've been awaiting your arrival for a lifetime. I'm so glad to be with you and grateful for the attention you're giving these words right now. Of course, you know there are NO accidents, right? So with just that knowledge under your belt, you're right where you're supposed to be, here with me!

I suspect you are a very powerful, energetic person. You are strong, persevering, determined and driven. And whether your demeanor is quiet and demure, or firm and forthright, you have the sense of knowing that there's so much more of you that has yet to come out. You have a certain level of awareness and realize that the greater potential in you is just waiting to burst forth. And that's why we're together.

Of course, you're probably asking yourself, "Okay, what is SHE going to tell me that I don't already know?" There is always some skepticism that ensues so let me share some of the training I've had. *The Power of Now* by Eckhart Tolle, *The Secret* by Rhonda Byrne, *The Power of Intention* by Wayne Dyer, and *The Dark Side of the Light Chasers* by Debbie Ford are just a few book titles that come to mind. I also received an Advanced Standing Master's Degree in Social Work in one year. I worked in an in-patient drug/alcohol treatment center doing therapy and groups. I've been in the field for close to 15 years working with all types. My clients' success rates hover at 98% and they swear they aren't the same people after working with me. If that transformation sounds like something you'd be interested in experiencing, please read on.

The benefits of my work with you are: understanding your internal energy field, learning how to quiet the mind, finding the on/off switch to the head, learning how to reconnect to the body/mind, becoming more in-tune and trusting of your intuition, releasing the resistant button, being present in "This Magic Moment", and magnetizing your empowerment with your own energy, within your body/mind, for the creation of your vision/goals.

As you can tell, there's a lot to cover, so let's get started. First, I'd like for you to get really present with these words. All words have a vibration to them. You can feel them within the body. In order for you to experience what I'm talking about, take your hands, place one on top of the other so the palms line up, and put them on your heart chakra, right in the upper-middle part of your chest. Then speak your name in a loud, low voice and feel the vibration from within your heart. Do it again, I want to make sure you are feeling this.

See, I told you'd get an experience from this. Say it again. You're heart chakra has five times more energy than your head. This heart chakra is your engine. It's where you create your intentions, your vision for what you want in your life. And a bit later I will explain to you the difference between intentions and affirmations ... Oh, that's part of being fully charged, by the way. Having fun yet? It's only going to get better! But let's start with the beginning ...

THIS MAGIC MOMENT

The number one thing that my clients deal with is how to stop the mind from thinking. They aren't sleeping, sometimes not eating, unable to focus, attention all over the place, and they just want relief. So when I share with them that I can teach them the on/off switch to the head, they laugh, "Oh yeah right!" Nothing they've done in the past, yoga, meditation, hypnosis, has worked. They think I'm pulling their leg. Of course, the ego/head would want them to think that because it loves the fact that it has control over them ... it's the mind-run-a-muck!! *Help Me Please!!* So I just let them know that the head, which is filled with doubt, fear, anger, ego, excuses, etc., will fight me. I've coined the phrase as the "Mental Mob Scene!" It has its own agenda, its tapes, and stories that keep it in charge. It will tell you how great you are at the same time it is tearing you into little pieces. It will lie to you and make you feel small and worthless. However, you have invested so much time and money into it, making it master over your universe that you think it's the end all/be all ... Well, it's time to teach it a thing or two. I call that "Train Your Brain."

Tony (name changed to protect the innocent!) came to me for the first time because he was going through a divorce, his career was suffering, his income way down, and he just didn't have enough energy to get out of bed. He was so stuck, and couldn't move—in a word, paralyzed. When he came in, his entire face was so white it was as if he were a ghost. I asked him to share his story with me, what was happening, if he had kids, what his life was like. He held his head in his hands and was on the verge of tears. I just listened as I was sending energy to him, holding him in an energetic cocoon. I asked him how he was feeling? What was happening in the body? He said, "I'm not feeling anything." I agreed—he was just numb. As with most men, he had a real fear around showing emotions. Some men will fight with all their will power, not to feel.

I shared with him that the first thing we have to do is get you out of your head. "Oh yeah, you bet, how are we going to do that?" I explained that it was very important for him to take command back from his head . . . that the head has been in control for some forty years and it's been doing a pretty good job of late, driving him crazy. "Yes, I know, okay let's go, I need to know this, hurry!" he said, rushed. I let him know that this was not going to be an easy task at first because the head doesn't not want to give up this controlling position that it's held for so long. I think he thought I was kidding. So, we began . . . after about 2 minutes, he just looked at me and said, "Are you kidding?" "Who's in charge here?" was my response. "I asked you to follow me, to let me lead you. I need for you to take charge of your energy, your attention and follow my instructions. Do you understand?" He was much more docile and relaxed, agreeing to listen, even though it was hard.

Within six minutes, he learned the tool, experienced at least three seconds of quiet for the very first time in his life. He was absolutely amazed. And then he began sharing from a completely different space, one that was calm, quiet, and responsive. We practiced a couple of more times, and each time he was able to extend the quiet moment, becoming more relaxed in his body, less anxious and so much more peaceful. By the time he left, his color was restored to his face; he was feeling lighter and had a new sense of energy, seeing what it was that he needed to do next. "This is a miracle!" he exclaimed. Yes, this is "The Magic Moment."

So let's begin. First, it takes about a second or two for the mind to create a story around what you are seeing. So, I'd like for you to find an object on your left-hand side and then find another object on your right-hand side. Of course, this works a lot better if I'm with you, guiding you, but right now I just want to you be aware, be a witness to your mind and watch it as you are doing this exercise. You'll be fascinated by how this little ol' mind of yours will fight, so I'm just issuing a little warning is all.

Now, as if you had a laser beam and you were directing it at that object, take your energy from the one object to the other every second or so. You want to be training the brain that you are the one in command, not it. Okay, one more thing, you direct your energy via your attention, so whatever you put your attention on, grows. So getting out of your head, you being in charge, I want you to shift back and forth on those two objects you choose. This is called "Shifting Your Energy." Don't stop because now I want you to be aware of the noise in your surroundings, just noticing without any mental opinion. Keep shifting your energy as you're aware of the noise, the hum of a refrigerator, the subtle noises outside, the sound of your breath, just be aware while you are still shifting your energy.

Then add to that, the tactile senses of touch . . . feel the clothes on your body. Feel the shoes on your feet, (if you have any on). Feel the pressure points where you're sitting, while you're still shifting your energy back and forth from one object to another and being aware of the sounds. Begin to slow down on shifting your attention from one side to another and notice the shadows on the walls, notice the lighting, just be aware. Take a deep breath, relax and just be present in "This Magic Moment." Let's face it, the only time you have is right now. You don't have a past, it's gone, and you have no idea whether you have a tomorrow or not. The only reality that exists is right now, and it's in this now moment that magic exists, hence the name, "This Magic Moment."

This Magic Moment allows you to wipe the slate clean, releasing yourself of the mental mob scene, the head battle, the control that the mind has on you. *Done!* You are now the one in command. You are in charge of where your mind goes, where you're going to put your energy, what you want to expand in your world. When you are in your head, your head is the one in control . . . boy, and it's such a control freak, no? Now, let's get really deep with this one— "You have NO control of anything, anyone, not even yourself!" Yep, you heard it here first, no "control" over a single thing. The mind would love to think that it does, will continue to manipulate you, to convince you that I'm wrong. It's okay; I expect it! But let's take a deeper look at this. First see what it feels like in the body when you think about "control." Notice all the times you tried to control someone, or better yet, when someone tried to control you. Can you feel the tightness or heaviness in the body? The usual, immediate, response is "No one's going to control me! You can't make me!!" See what I mean? There's a physical sensation in the body. It doesn't feel good! And just notice how with control, there's also resistance. Whatever you resist, persists. Guaranteed! It's the golden rule. And what's more, when you resist anything you put so much attention/ energy on it from your negativity, which you bring it right to you. Remember, you're a magnet. It's like two magnets that repulse each other, you're trying to push it away, pretend it's not there, you're just not going to feel it no matter what, but with all that energy on it, you are bringing in the negativity like an onslaught to sabotage you which eventually will have consequences that can present in a physical form, or an emotional experience. Or maybe, you just plain beat yourself up. Whichever, you will resist yourself right into it . . . *Whammo!!*

FEELINGS VERSUS EMOTIONS

For at least the last 25 years we've been hearing from all sorts of self-help gurus, therapist, counselors, psychologists, "What does that feel like?" It became the new language of expressing oneself in order to resolve conflicts, speak what was on an individual's mind, and move forward in a relationship without the other person feeling attacked or offended. It was safe speaking ground in order to get your point across and create change. Unfortunately there were many who were not comfortable with their emotions and would shut down. "No thank you, I'm not going there." And of course, as in this society, men were very comfortable with keeping their emotions inside, as they were never allowed to expresses them. The only thing that was allowed was their anger.

However, and this is BIG, we do EVERYTHING based on a feeling. Everything that we do is either to feel more of this or not to feel that!! And here's the dichotomy . . . we do everything based on feeling, yet we don't want to feel. Talk about a yoyo of energy. And boy, do we feel that too. I want you to tap your finger on your leg . . . feel it? It's a physical sensation, a feeling. A feeling can have emotions attached to them. So another little exercise . . . "If you believe you can, or you believe you can't, YOU'RE RIGHT!!! What do you believe? So put all your energy on the words "I Can." What does that feel like? Identify the feeling within the body/mind. This is a critical question because most people are living their lives based on what they THINK they should feel, not on experiencing their lives through their energy field.

Now, once you've identified where in the body that sensation lives—mine is usually in my back and shoulders— it feels like strength to me, then put all your energy/attention in that place in my body and feel it, and feel it even more, because whatever we put our energy/attention on grows. Keep growing it now. Can you feel it expanding in the body? Excellent job! This is so important because we all want to feel good, strong, courageous, invincible, joyful and more. The more you take these words and feel them in the body, magnetizing the feeling, the more their vibration expands internally, and the more you create and attract from that field. Like energy begets like. Oh, guess what? That's one more FULLY CHARGED insight to creating. It's not a head job, think, think, think and more thinking . . . it's all about the feelings, feeling it in the body, believing it without a doubt. Oh, and this is good too, the only place doubt lives is in the head! So get into your Magic Moment!

IT'S ALL AN INSIDE JOB

What an interesting concept, "It's all an inside job." What does that really mean? It means that there are certain beliefs that we hold near and dear and they can be positive or negative in nature. There are also beliefs that are working subconsciously because we have pretty much buried them, we don't want to think about them and they don't make us feel good so we deny them, pretend they aren't affecting us, etc. Well, guess again! They do follow us, they become a pattern in our lives and even though the characters and stories might change, the pattern of the belief stays the same.

So we go through life taking on others' beliefs while building upon our own . . . what to do, what not to do, what to say, how to say it. We shame ourselves for saying this or that . . . and life becomes a big headache, literally. And here's the really big awakening, we always see evidence for our beliefs, always. Example: Let's go back to the belief that if you can, then there will be all sorts of evidence to prove to you, wow, I can . . . *and* it has a physical sensation in the body. This belief, an empowerment belief, feels good and comes from a high vibrational frequency. The same thing goes if you believe you can't. You will again, physically feel the sensation of that belief. It could be a heavy feel inside the body, or droopy shoulders, head hanging down, whatever it is, that belief elicits a very low energy vibration.

Now, if there's something you don't believe, you won't see it. It's not going to appear. Not unless you change your beliefs around it. And guess what, you can! You can do anything you want . . . and you can tell your head what you're going to believe. Don't let the mental mob scene have that kind of control. You have to take back command of it and let it know who is boss. Who's in charge? Listen, I'm going to let you in on a little secret . . .

YOU ARE NOT YOUR THOUGHTS

You are not your thoughts; you have thoughts. Many of us believe that our mind is the absolute control center of our entire beingness. Well gang, I'm here to tell you, that ain't so. How often can you stop and listen to what's going on in your head? And who's aware of that? It's outside of your mind. Oh my, what am I saying? Okay, hold on . . . there's a much more powerful part of you that is aware. It just kind of sits there and watches. It's not in judgment, it's not commenting; however every now and then it says, "Hello?" What are you saying to yourself? You know better, why are you listening to all that nonsense going on in that head of yours? We usually start out with a conversation in our head, of course, then we will engage other people's voices with ours, then we will have an argument about what was said, what wasn't said, how it was said, what you should have said but didn't and now you look like an idiot because you didn't . . . Sound familiar? Oh my, it's the mental mob scene at play once more.

There's another *Aha* moment; you have emotions but you are not your emotions. Oh gosh, another Aha moment; the feeling lasts no more than 10 minutes at the most. It's when we go up into our heads, putting all our energy up there, that suffering occurs. And that will glue you right onto that memory for days, years, even decades. Geez, some people are still holding grudges against another, suffering, even after they're dead and buried! Here's the trick with that, remember, don't resist anything, just feel it, experience it. See where it is in the body and take a deep breath into that energy contraction, a slow deep breath all the way in and all the way out. Do that again and relax into the contraction. Now from that neutral observer self, just notice the contraction, without any judgment on it, just noticing it with neutral energy. Neutral Energy from that Aware Observer within you is another term for unconditional love. Unconditional love means there is no agenda working, no conditions that have to be met, there is just pure radiant energy/attention being given to the feeling. And before you know it, it's gone. You've neutralized it! And once neutralized, you no longer have to create/attract from that contraction, from that lower vibrational frequency. Remember, like energy begets like. You are a magnet. So, here's another golden nugget, as I'd like to call the power of receiving.

THE POWER OF RECEIVING

It being a fact that we have electromagnetic energy running through us, it's imperative that we receive. Are you a giver? Give, give, give until you run dry. Then you look for the people that you've given to, to give back to you . . . but they don't. And you keep waiting, while you're still giving tirelessly and before you know it, you're getting irritated, frustrated, and angry because you have set yourself up with expectations from those other people on how, when, and why they should be giving back to you.

Well, here's how to tell . . . how good are you at taking a compliment? Receiving a gift? Being praised? If any of these things make you cringe, you are not allowing yourself to receive. I'm not talking about ego here, I'm talking about sincerely receiving the compliment and thanking the individual for it. How easy is it for you just to say thank you from your heart and feel it inside? Now, there are many different facets of this situation . . . and that's why it's going to be so important for you to get this. You cannot give what you don't have. Everything that you give has energy to it. If you don't receive, you don't have enough energy to continuously give; you get depleted. Oh, then you go up into the head and start the battle about why you're giving, who should be giving back to you, and your energy level dips even further. Do this little exercise. It will make my point. Take a deep breath and exhale, exhale some more, exhale even more, no you can't take a breath, exhale more . . . Okay, when are you going to receive? If you can't allow the universe to give back to you, you will never have enough breath for any kind of life! Bottom line!

Another reason to receive is that you give the other person the ability of receiving as well. Remember, it's the mirroring effect. The more you accept, the more you give others outside of yourself permission to accept. You've also honored the gift and the givers feel good about themselves.

This pattern can clear itself up easily. When someone gives you a compliment, allow yourself to feel it and just say thank you. It's that easy. Oh, here's another nugget, the people that you were waiting to give back to you, probably have been. But when you can't receive, their gifts fall to the ground. Really, ask yourself, why can't I accept? What do I really believe about myself that won't allow me to receive? You'll notice that there is a disempowering belief at the root of it. And it's usually our core issue.

One of the biggest complaints I hear is "I'm not deserving, not good enough." As we have grown up, our messages that we've internalized from our authority figures were mostly negative. "Don't do this, stop that, what's wrong with you, are you stupid or what, when are you ever going to learn," and the list goes on. We take these beliefs on as our own because at this young age we look up to these authority figures and believe what they are telling us. We don't know any better. And every time we get reprimanded this belief becomes whom we believe we are. I don't know about you, but my messages were pretty clear about not being good enough: *Little girls should be seen, not heard.* And I grew up trying so hard to prove that I was worthy, that I was good enough and that I could be somebody.

With those tapes going on inside our heads, the suffering and struggling that we go through feels insurmountable. For quite some time, I had a mild depression, was never really happy, and always played "less than" in one way or another. As we age, these tapes get louder and louder. The beliefs play themselves out because that's the ingenious way we have in seeing and experiencing where our wounds are. This is called . . .

THE MIRRORING EFFECT

There's a wonderful analogy that was shared by David Icke that goes like this: You don't like what you see out there in the external world so you go up to the mirror, you're watching all that stuff in the mirror, and you pick up the comb wanting to change what you see and begin to comb the mirror. And it doesn't work, so you pick up the brush and brush the mirror and that doesn't work either. Notice how we are always trying to control events, people, and situations outside of ourselves looking for the reflection to be different. Well, it doesn't work that way. It's all an inside job! The only way the view in the mirror is going to change is if you comb/brush your own hair.

Gandhi had been saying this for years, and we say it now, even after he's gone, "Be the change you wish to see in the world!"

Through the healing of the internal, the external reaps the benefits of what life has to offer. And here's another Aha moment—you can't control a thing! No person, no nothing! Zip. Nada. Squat. Not even yourself. You may think you can and the operative word here is *think*, but all someone has to do is look at you a certain way or say a word, and you're off and running, not controlling a darn thing! And that's when you give your power away. You've given it right to them to do with what they want . . . and they are usually looking at messing you up, because NO ONE wants to be controlled. Got it? It's all an external power-play of control and manipulation that, my friends, creates an emotional charge within your energy field. You can physically feel it! And that emotional charge will set off sparks. Those sparks create a jolt in the body and before you know it, you'll be ready for battle. I call them the hot buttons, let someone just say or look at you the wrong way, and you will attack.

What's amazing is that through the reflection of another we can see our wounds, what needs to be healed. You couldn't recognize what it is that you don't like in another unless it lived in you first. Here's a great analogy, someone lies to you, you get angry and feel betrayed. However, where have you lied to someone (not necessary to the same person, it doesn't matter), but more importantly, look to see where you've lied to yourself. There's a boomerang effect . . . because it's all an inside job. *Period.*

Clean up within yourself what is out of integrity. Are you clear, concise, and honest in your communications with others? Do you follow through on what you say? Do you gossip about others making yourself feel better at someone's expense? Just ask yourself, "What kind of person would do that to another? Or would not honor their word?" When you are out of integrity, you create and attract others that are out of their integrity. Like energy begets like, remember? It's really that simple . . . lie and you attract and create liars. Steal and you'll create and attract thieves. Judge another and you'll be judged. This is the law that has been told to us over and over again. You reap what you sow or what goes around comes around. There is much truth in these sayings. This vibrational frequency is very destructive and will continue self-sabotaging behaviors which will then lead to beating yourself up, creating the mental mob scene, feeling guilty and shameful . . . And as you know, the guilty always seek punishment. Another golden nugget: ask where you are punishing yourself? And why would you do that to yourself? It doesn't feel good; it hurts. Ouch! Enough! It's now time to learn how to . . .

SHIFT YOUR ENERGY

Wherever you put your energy/attention, it grows. If you are stuck in your head beating yourself up about past mistakes or so over consumed by what your future will look like, there is no possible way that you could be in the present moment, This Magic Moment. Your energy is fragmented and scattered. Distraction seems to be common today and people are pulling your attention everywhere . . . and nothing is getting done. All your energy is in your disempowerment, your lack and limitations, which then grow and become overwhelming. And because you don't want to feel that discomfort, you run back up in your head and try to figure out what to do next, confusion sets in and before you know it, the stress is driving you crazy. And stress is the number one killer.

So, get into "This Magic Moment," being present and in the NOW moment. Then shift your energy into what it is that you do want to feel. Create a memory that has given you love and joy, allow the experience of that time to embrace you, and feel in the body/mind where those feeling live. Be deliberate with your energy and don't let your mind take off with you. Now, with all your energy directed to that place in your body, *intensify it*, really feel it even more. This is an important part of the process of manifesting because you want to magnetize that feeling in your body. It will create and attract more of the same at that higher vibrational frequency which in turn really feels good. And all we want is to feel good. Aren't you tired of feeling bad, pushing away all the negative tapes that just keep going on and on? Shift your energy and begin loving life once more. Shift your energy and start experiencing life. Shift your energy and release yourself from the onslaught of negativity. Shift your energy and improve the quality of your life. Shift your energy and live the life you're always wanted. Shift your energy and transform your life!

INTENTION VERSUS AFFIRMATIONS

For many of us saying affirmations has been a way of life. Louise Hay was one of the gurus of this practice, based on her book "Heal Your Body" which for many is a Bible. Affirmations were a good tool, however with the advent of quantum physics, we now have the discovery of how attention/energy is the driving force creating our life experiences in the external energy grid. Understanding the heart energy is another breakthrough area. According to "HeartMath," researchers have measured the energy field surrounding us as a 360 degree circle, starting from the heart, radiating outside of us by, at least, 10 feet. So learning how to direct our energy is vital. Eckhart Tolle's *The Power of Now* tells us that the only time we have is now, yesterdays are gone, and no one knows if we have any tomorrows . . . All we have is right *NOW*. Oh, and let's not forget Wayne Dyer's *The Power of Intention* which helps with another piece of the puzzle in the process of manifesting.

So, let's connect the dots. Shall we say, with the heart, the engine, at the starting point of the energy, get present in this now moment, quiet the mind, shift your energy/attention into your heart and feel it growing/expanding. As we did in the beginning of this chapter, put your right palm on your heart chakra, place your left palm on top of the right and then speak your name loud and deep, like you were talking from your heart. Feel the vibration? Say it again so you can experience the physical sensation of the words. Now let's create an affirmation based on your vision. Start your intention with the most powerful words of "I AM" and state it in the present tense. Example: *I AM Now Ready To Receive My Success*. Another could be, *I AM Healthy, Happy, And Joyful In All My Relationships*. Say it out loud and feel the vibration of your intention in your heart engine and keep feeling it. Being that you are all energy, a magnet, you want to put all your energy into that engine and build that magnet of your intention. And why would you want to do this?

THE MIRACLES OF MANIFESTING

Anytime we encounter change, the first thing that happens is resistance. Then the ego/head starts creating excuses for staying stuck. Instead of looking for the negative, I'd like for you to experience the positive. Fear keeps us stuck in the space of sameness, predictability, and stagnation. It's when you step into the "unknown" that growth happens opening you up to the possibilities that make you feel exhilarated. This inner joy is where you experience courage, determination, untapped talents, and a power inside of you never before experienced. In that space is where miracles happen.

I remember back about three years ago, I made a decision to move to Fort Lauderdale from Orlando. I had a beautiful home with all the amenities, two dogs and thriving businesses in both coaching and real estate. However, I wanted to expand my knowledge and use other talents to enhance my coaching business via additional studies. I had my home up for sale for eight months with no successful offers. I was asked if I would be open to renting out my home. I did the math, did meditation, set my intentions and after just 48 hours, I had a rental contract . . . a miracle. Two days later I was in Fort Lauderdale. I didn't know the area so I had set an appointment for a realtor to show me around. I intended and felt what I wanted, a condo near the water, pet friendly, with a view! Last minute she cancelled so I decided to drive around and feel out the location. I was drawn to this pink high-rise building. I sat in front of it watching the tenants come and go, noticing their demeanor, their age, and of course, if there were any dogs in the picture. I was also feeling the community, what was the energy?

After about five minutes, I could feel a wonderful vibration, I enjoyed watching the people. They were young professionals, full of life. So I proceeded inside and asked the lobby security guard if there were any apartments for rent. Oh, but first, do they accept dogs? He sat there looking at me then looked around the corner and said, "Maybe she can help you." There, coming up the walkway, was a real estate agent. I created an agent right there when I needed her. When she came in, I introduced myself to her and she looked confused. I told her I was looking for either a one or two bedroom and she shared that she was previewing an apartment for another client of hers. So I accompanied her upstairs to see a beautiful, large, redone condo that sat on the water, where boats would go by and music played in the restaurants across from me. And the rent was negotiated within my budget, so I took it . . . *Miracle!* And those miracles haven't stopped.

MY WISH FOR YOU!

My wish, my desire, my passion is that you have everything you want in life, whatever that may be. To experience life FULLY CHARGED, sharing your greatness with the world, and loving with abandonment. You have everything it takes to be more than you've ever believed possible. So I challenge you to use these tools, apply them in your everyday life, share them with others, and make that positive impact on all that you touch. Shift Your Energy, Transform Your Life. Create, Feel, Experience Your Vision Now! Because you are a FULLY CHARGED MIRACLE!

MICHELLE STRAKA is the chef/owner of Golden Plate Catering in Plantation Florida. She is also a certified trainer who specializes in boxing and women's self-defense. On July 29, 2011, Michelle left her job as an Executive Chef at Aramark Corporation to pursue her passion in health and fitness. She opened up Golden Plate Catering which specializes in healthy catering and pre-packaged meals.

Michelle is also a second-degree black belt in Tae Kwon Do who trained for 15 years under Grandmaster Sung Wuk Chung, a world champion and ninth degree black belt. In addition to Golden Plate Catering, she works with Dialed in Fitness teaching boxing, weights, and self-defense. She empowers others by showing them that, "Yes You Can".

DEDICATION

I would like to dedicate "Lights Out" to the Glorious Being Center. Poverty doesn't discriminate in this world and The Glorious Being Center realizes this. They help to educate and build centers for the children of Ghana, Africa. The GB Center has made great strides, one step at a time.

Chapter Nine

Lights Out
by Michelle Straka

Standing in the center of the ring, with my tightly gloved hands held high, the announcer, proclaimed, "The winner, by unanimous decision, in the red corner, Michelle, 'The Machine,' Straka." I did it! I overcame one of my biggest fears and shocked the boxing world at the same time.

I stepped into the ring as the obvious underdog and came out the 2006 140lb Division Heroes in Action Champion. I was specifically chosen for this fight. No, not because I was the most talented boxer, on the contrary, I was chosen . . . to lose. My opponent, Pam "Bam Bam" Bradley was a former Golden Gloves champ who had a lot more fight experience than I did. Not only was this my first fight, it was held at one of South Florida's premier boxing venues, the Seminole Hard Rock in front of 2,000 people and covered on the local NBC station and Telemundo. Beyond that, sitting in my corner with the former owner of my gym was Angelo Dundee, the American Boxing Cornerman. Dundee is famous for his work with 15 world champions including Muhammad Ali, Sugar Ray Leonard and George Foreman, to name a few. Talk about pressure.

Winning this fight was a huge turning point in my life. The training alone made me a stronger, more disciplined person both mentally and physically. This was one of the biggest challenges of my life and because of it, I learned a lot about myself.

I started training seriously in June, 3 months before that fight. I trained with the amateur team and wasn't really serious about it. I was boxing because it helped alleviate the stress I dealt with day in and day out as an executive chef. And, at 36, I was the oldest one on the team. An amateur's average age is only 19.

My coach, Dave Marks, approached me one day at the boxing gym where I train in May, 2006. I had only been dabbling in boxing for about a year. Coach asked me if I wanted to fight at the Hard Rock that September. "For real?" I said with disbelief. "Hell yeah," he said, "I believe you can fight." I couldn't believe that I was going to achieve my dream. Fighting at the Hard Rock was something I've always dreamed about but never thought I could do. I had every excuse in the book as to why I would never be a champion, the biggest of which is that I had absolutely no confidence in myself. Coach Dave explained, "Listen, this isn't gonna be a cakewalk. You're gonna have to work and work hard." "I don't mind work," I said, "I can work, it's getting killed that worries me!" "That's where I come in," he said proudly, "You'll have to train like it's a 10 round title fight." So even though I was scared, my stomach churning and my heart racing, I committed to do it. With a satisfied smile, Coach Dave said, "Good, I'll see you right after you get off work tomorrow."

I had no idea how much energy I was going to have to put into this. Every day until the fight I was up at before 4:00am to be at work by 5, driving 45 minutes to an hour to get there. After I put in a full day of running a fast-paced kitchen with 15 employees, I'd leave work around 3:00 drive 90 minutes to the gym and train for another hour and half. Then I'd head home, dead tired about 7:00. Typically I'd eat dinner and then go out for a minimum 2 mile run. Coach Dave usually called around 10:30 and we'd go over the day's training. Weekends were 3-hour gym days followed by my nightly run. I never in my wildest dreams thought I could train this hard, but I was determined not to let down the man who actually had enough faith in me to think I could compete and was willing to train me, my coach. I had a dream, but without the help of Coach Dave I would not be where I am today. He took me under his wing and dedicated hours, days and months of his time to make me the best I could be.

One day at work I got a phone call from Coach Dave saying, "Get your sparring gear and get over to Hollywood P.A.L. by 5:00. You're sparring with Pam "Bam Bam" Bradley." I had to try out for the Heroes in action fight at the Hard Rock.

My drive to the P.A.L. seemed endless. My knees knocked, my hands shook, and I couldn't eat a thing. The event coordinator, a good friend of Coach Dave, had Pam and I go first. I never shook so hard in my life. My mouth guard gagged me and my helmet gave me claustrophobia, but I still climbed into the ring.

The bell rang and Bam Bam jumped on me like a bat out of hell. I forgot everything but instinct. My instinct was to survive and I did. The tryouts were awful for me. I bruised my ribs sparring. All I did was survive. This didn't faze Coach at all. He told me, "We're gonna surprise everyone." With conviction he said, "You can beat that girl." I was happy to have survived sparring with Pam. She opened my eyes with her aggression. I was scared as hell, but I could not let

Coach down. He really believed that I could beat this girl. So I had to believe it too.

I spent the next 2 months training, running, sparring, and working full-time. To top that off, Coach and I ended up doing a lot of media interviews to promote the Hard Rock fight. We were featured in the Miami Herald, on NBC 6, Telemundo and various other newspapers and magazines. The media attention put more pressure on me to win. I felt that I had to work harder to meet everyone's expectations.

About a month before the big fight I hit the proverbial wall. I was exhausted and couldn't go on anymore. My body ached, I couldn't get enough sleep and I was angry all the time.

Sparring one Saturday with the coach, I couldn't get anything right. My punches were slow and timid. I stood in front of him and kept getting hit. I didn't have the energy to hit back. I wasn't doing what I was told. He screamed for me to extend the jab and follow through on my punches. But I was so tired I couldn't lift my arms any longer. He reached a point where he literally pushed me to the floor of the ring and asked me if I was a fighter or a quitter. Frustrated with my lack of effort and my obvious unwillingness to get beyond my physical and mental wall, he looked me straight in the eye and said, "I don't train quitters." From that point on I was determined to find the strength to pull myself up and train like a champion.

The week before the fight was the time to get my strength back and let my body heal. Now it was a mental game. I was so wired up I couldn't sleep and ended up swallowing Tylenol PM. The littlest thing would set me off. A guy cut me off one day, while I was driving. I jumped out of truck and almost beat the crap out of him. He was lucky I wasn't allowed to fight.

The day of the fight I focused on trying to relax. It was hard to do so with my mind going at the speed of light. I felt like I had the whole world on my shoulders. Although people were around, I felt alone. Nobody could relate to what I was going through. I was anxious, angry, and sick to my stomach. I wanted to run away and never come back. It would have been easy just to quit. I was afraid of the unknown. Boxing is a dangerous sport. Many fighters have lost their lives in the ring. All I could visualize now was that my dream was actually coming true. I visualized in my mind the entire fight. I kept telling myself that I was going to jump on this girl at the bell and never let up. I visualized this in my mind until the actual fight.

Visualization is the key to being successful. I would visualize myself being relaxed now just as I'd been visualizing myself winning the fight. I truly believe that if I had not visualized winning the fight, it wouldn't have happened. Period. To this day, I use visualization in everything I do. If I'm speaking, I visualize successfully delivering my speech. If I'm catering an event, I picture in my mind how everything should look, smell and taste.

The best way to be effective with this technique is to sit down, close your eyes and visualize your goals. See them in your mind. Start with a small goal, such as what your perfect day should look like. Then move on to your dream career, house, financial, and personal goals. I've disciplined myself to meditate 15 minutes in the morning and 15 minutes at night before bed. During these meditations, I use my technique to organize my day and visualize my goals. Visualization works, but only if you take action and persevere. The formula for success is:

Visualization + Perseverance + Action = Success.

A year and a half ago, I set a goal to compete and win in the Women's National Golden Gloves, which was to be held that summer, 4 months later. I had originally competed in the Golden Gloves in the previous year, but ended up with the third seed in my division. I walked away with a bronze medal and a third place ranking in the country. Most people would be happy with this, but I had not completely accomplished my goal.

After that first attempt at a Golden Gloves championship I continued to train. I still hadn't achieved my goal of winning. I got a phone call from the Hollywood P.A.L., asking me to compete again in the "Heroes in Action," the same tournament at the Hard Rock where I successfully beat "Bam-Bam." Of course, I said yes. I was pumped and ready to go. There was one problem; they put me up against my friend and teammate, Danielle Moratta. My coach was beside himself. Being on the same team meant we had the same coach and corner man, Coach Dave. He couldn't work the corner for both of us at the same time. Thank goodness he could still coach us both. Because we were teammates and sparred together often, we knew each other's strengthens and weaknesses inside and out. How was I going to beat her when she knew all my strategies? Lucky for me I had ten pounds on her. Lucky for her, she had ten years of youth on me. Her punches were much quicker than mine, but I could move my head much faster.

Coach Dave found a professional fighter and coach he used to train to work Danielle's corner. He worked mine. Because I didn't train as hard for this fight as my previous one, I wasn't as nervous for this fight. The night of the fight, I was relaxed without a care in the world. Danielle was quiet and focused.

We were both introduced and we stepped into the ring. The bell rang and it was "game on." Well, I should say, it was "game on" for Danielle. She jumped out of her corner and exploded on me like a firecracker. I was just given my wakeup call! I survived the first round. I don't know how, but I did. The bell rang again; I was up and after her. I won the second round. I was gassed and I wore her out with my weight.

The third and final round began. The two of us started throwing our hands, but we were both exhausted. The problem was, she was mentally stronger than I was. She forced herself to throw punches when I couldn't. The bell rang. She won. She deserved the win. I am grateful for this wake up call. It goes to show that even with the best effort you still have to be ready to adjust what you're doing to reach your intended target. This was a lesson learned for me. I had not followed my formula. I fought a great fight, but because I had not mentally prepared myself, I did not succeed. How could I compete in the Golden Gloves and win if I am going to fight like that? I would not let this happen again.

I continued more training. I trained for months. Two months before the Golden Gloves fight, I injured what I thought was my left wrist. It turned out to be a tendon in my elbow. The orthopedic doctor put me in an arm brace and told me no boxing for 6 months. I said okay to him but didn't follow anything he said. I had a goal to complete. I wore my arm brace at work, but took it off before I arrived at the gym. If I had told my coach, he would tell me not to fight. It was easier to try to hide it. Every time I hit the mitts or the heavy bags, I wanted to cry. The pain was intense, but I had to complete my goal. I gritted my teeth and swallowed the pain. I would not complete my goal by letting the injury control my life. This was just another bump in the road.

Sparring one afternoon a few months before the fight, I was hit in my chin and lost my legs. The hit left me dazed. I ended up with a concussion. Coach was so upset and worried, he asked me to quit competing. He wanted to train me, but just for exercise. I was crushed. I couldn't believe he was doing this to me. I now understand that he was just looking out for me. Still, at the time, I was in a rage. I found another trainer, José Perez. He was a guy I used to box with. We both started boxing about the same time. At one time, he trained under Coach Dave. The two of us used to spar together. The only problem I had was his age. He's about ten years younger than me. When we used to train, he was irresponsible. He was always late to practice and liked to live the good life. I decided to give him a chance, because I needed to accomplish my goal.

I began training again. José surprised me. He began working on hand and foot speed. I struggled with it at first but surprisingly picked it up quickly. This was good since the fight was right around the corner.

The fight was scheduled the night before the start of the Gloves Championship. No one showed up in my weight class, so I was scheduled to fight a girl in a heavier weight class. There was a problem. I weighed 132 pounds and she weighed 156 pounds. In order to fight, I had to get up to at least 137 pounds and she had to drop down to 150 pounds. I went home and drank everything I could find. I know that she went straight to the sauna. This was to my advantage. She would be dehydrated. I would be fully hydrated and at full strength. The next morning, I weighed in at 137 lbs. and she barely made 150 lbs. The fight was on. We both successfully completed our first obstacle. Now we just had to wait for the evening to fight.

The night of the fight, I got there and looked around but no coach. José was 3 hours late. Can you believe it? Okay, finally he was there. I told myself not to worry about the fight. As he was wrapping my hands, I came to find out that he hadn't renewed his coaches' license, which means that he couldn't work my corner. I was fired up and not at my opponent. I was going to kill this man! I was angry by the time my fight began; I knocked this girl down within the first thirty seconds of the round.

The bad thing was she was so much bigger than I was, so she got back up. And I suddenly noticed this girl was huge. I had to keep moving around the ring so she couldn't catch me. I had to hit and run. All she had to do was lay on me and I would tire out. I would not have completed my goal if I hadn't had hand and foot speed. The fact that I did meant that my training with José had paid off.

I was able to accomplish my goal. I became the 2010 National Golden Gloves Champion – Master's 140lb Division.

I used to think that I was the luckiest person in the world. I thought that my accomplishments were all brought about by luck. Now I look back and realize that all my success was earned. I sat down one day and thought about how I have made myself successful. It was by using that same formula over and over again.

Jack Canfield states in "*The Success Principles*," "Visualization, or the act of creating compelling and vivid pictures in your mind, may be the most underutilized success tool you possess, because it greatly accelerates the achievements of any success in three powerful ways." Visualization, Perseverance, and Taking Action work, *but they all work together*. This combination equals "Lights Out" if used together.

The lessons I learned about persistence and overcoming fear continues to help me every single day in all aspects of my life. I've recently taken the plunge from being an executive chef at a company with a steady job, to creating my own catering company. I was driving in my car one day and an idea hit me. I had a vision for healthy catering and pre-packaged meals under 500 calories. My passion in life has always been health and nutrition. I watched my family members get sick and die from obesity. From there, I sat in the morning before work and before bed to visualize what my menu would consist of. I pictured what my food looked and tasted like. I even visualized my logo.

Once I visualized my dream, I wrote down the ideas and took action. Goldenplate Catering was born out of my vision but only because I took action. Visualization is a powerful tool that works, but if I did not go through the grueling training and actually fight in the ring, it would not have worked. Was I scared? Yes. Did I do it anyway? Yes, because I knew it was the right thing for me; I knew I could do anything I decided to do. All it would take to create a catering success was the same commitment, dedication, and action I've taken to accomplish any other goal.

Leaving a secure job with a steady paycheck was one of the scariest things I've ever done. If it wasn't for boxing and for Coach Dave giving me the confidence to hold my head up high, I might not have taken that step. I learned how to persevere and get what I want. Leaving my job was no different from stepping into the ring; it took a dream and it took determination. And being successful in my business takes the same persistence, the same commitment and the same hard work as becoming a Golden Gloves Champion. I have to be willing to do what it takes, no matter what.

To this day, I sit down in the morning before I start my cardio, and read my goals and affirmations. Once I'm on the treadmill, I visualize those goals and dreams. This process has an added side benefits; I get lots of great ideas while I'm on the treadmill. One morning while I was walking on the treadmill, training for my first bodybuilding show, out of nowhere came the song and start of the 90-second routine for my show. Oh, did I forget to mention I'm a bodybuilder now? I dove into bodybuilding because I've always been envious of how those athletes look. I met a female bodybuilder last year and she inspired me to try it. I met her on Saturday and was in action right away, at her gym talking to her trainer, Julio Hernandez, the following Monday. I never looked back from there.

I got in the creative flow and envisioned my moves for each part of the song and how I would look. Since I was brand new to Bodybuilding and unfamiliar with the poses and routines, this challenge was a real breakthrough for me. Once I had the routine in my head, I showed my trainer the idea. I was embarrassed showing him, because I have no experience in bodybuilding, but I did it anyway. He couldn't believe how great it was. He loved it.

I was psyched up. It was one of the greatest ideas I've had. With my knowledge of boxing and his experience with bodybuilding, we blended boxing and bodybuilding together. It worked! I took first place in the middleweight division and second place in the over 40 division. Not bad for my first time ever.

The amazing thing is that it was a qualifying show. Most bodybuilders do not qualify at their first show. This show was a level 5, which is the highest amateur bodybuilding show that you can participate in besides The Nationals. Needless to say, I qualified for Master's Nationals in July 2012. My next goal is to compete in and win the Master's Nationals.

As I'm writing this, I'm already visualizing what I'll look like and how I'll pose. I have my first show under my belt, so I have a better idea of what I need to do. I learned that I need to be thicker for my height and that I need to tighten my hamstrings. I visualize what I want my body to look like. To be a champion, adjustments such as these must be made in order to better your self.

Now that I see myself competing in Nationals, I must take action and persevere. A win at Nationals isn't going to be handed to me. I'm going to have to work for it. Like anything worth having, winning Nationals is going to demand 8 months of tenacity, 8 months of doing whatever it takes, 8 months of being willing to pay the price. There's going to be continuous strict dieting and cardio. My diet will be limited to 25-75grms of carbohydrates daily. I will be eating mostly white fish and fresh vegetables. There will be no sugar in my diet. Cardio will consist of three hours a day on the treadmill.

I'll be lifting weights every day. I usually lift one body part a day. On top of that, I'll still be running Goldenplate Catering and training my personal fitness clients.

I'm confident that I will succeed and be crowned as the women's middleweight body building champ at Nationals. You too can have that same confidence, that same belief in yourself and you too can achieve *anything* you want in your life. It's all in your hands. With persistence, dedication, consistent action and the willingness to give up what others wouldn't, you can achieve anything you choose to. Now get to it. *It's your life!* Make it everything you want it to be!

KATHY DEDEK inspires business owners to create extraordinary companies. Her knowledge spans across sales, marketing, technology, accounting and business management. She has mentored with some of the best, including Michael Gerber, author of The *E-Myth* and 9 other books and AmondaRose Igoe, author of *Pain-Free Presentations*.

Kathy is nationally recognized as a contributing author of *Visionaries With Guts* (2010) where she reveals how a company can become the next Disney. She is co-author of *The Ultimate Success Secret – South Florida Edition* (2011), has appeared in *The Sun Sentinel* and was featured in the Technology section of *In-Focus Magazine*.

As a sought after speaker, with audiences of 5 to 500 people. Her topics range from creating client value, setting client expectations, building effective sales strategies, andgetting paid before you do the work. One of her favorite presentations, The Money is in the

Follow-up, was when she shared the stage three years ago with Bob Burg, John Di Lemme, Loral Langemeier and Nancy Matthews.

Kathy has spoken to audiences such as the National Association of Women Business Owners (NAWBO), the Business Network International's (BNI) Regional Conference, the Women's Prosperity Network Expo, the Women's Power Caucus, American Express, Waste Management, Sun Bank and the City of Fort Lauderdale.

Kathy is the CEO and Founder of Shattering the Glass, Inc. (STG). Shattering the Glass™ was conceived in the Dreaming Room, led by Michael Gerber. This experience had such a profound impact on her that she attented 2 more Dreaming Room workshops and became a certified facilitator. She leads her audience to discover the dream inside them, and then teaches each participant how to build a successful business around that dream, the right way, the first time.

Kathy is married to Bill Dedek, sharing the helm of her sales and technology company, Brilliant Technology Applied(BTA™). Her daughter, Haley Orr, a junior at Florida State University in Tallahassee and is the Vice President of Shattering the Glass, Inc.

Contact Kathy Dedek

www.kathydedek.com

954-644-2662

kathy@bta4sales.com

DEDICATION

I dedicate my chapter to my father, Al Mackey. You taught me how to live and to laugh, but most of all you gave me a love for sales. I want to share this feeling with everyone in hopes that they will learn to love it too. Thank you, Daddy.

Chapter Ten

Closing the Gap
by Kathy Dedek

Selling. Some people like it; others dread it like the plague. Whether you like it or not, the truth is most people don't feel comfortable selling, even the ones that like to sell. I am going to show you how you can close this gap and make selling easy.

I like selling, it is in my blood. You see, my father was a salesman. Not in the pushy kind of way, but he knew how to pay attention and always gave the customer what they wanted with very little effort on his part. He taught me how to make selling enjoyable. I want to pass this knowledge on to you. I hope that you too can enjoy the selling process and feel at ease with offering your products and services to buyers.

Most people learn best by doing. Remember when you were young and learning how to tie your tennis shoes. At first you weren't very good at it. The loops never matched. The laces came undone. But you were determined to tie your own shoes. So you practiced when no one was looking and then one day it happened. You tied your shoes and they stayed tied!

Now you don't even think about it when you put on your tennis shoes. You just tie them. Like on autopilot.

What if you could apply the same success to sales? Selling would become so simple that you just did it naturally and never really thought about it, like tying your shoes.

So how can you sell effortlessly? How can you close the gap between Contact and Contract? How do you learn to approach sales like tying your shoes?

The answer is by developing a customer buying process. Focusing your attention directly on the buyer and away from you, the seller, drastically improves the prospect's experience and makes it easier for you to sell your products and services.

I am Kathy Dedek and half of Brilliant Technology Applied™. My business partner and husband, Bill Dedek, is the other half. Together we help business owners create buyers. Our series of workshops and training classes help businesses create a "Buyer Zone". But they didn't start out that way in the beginning.

In my book, *The Ultimate Success Secret* with Dan Kennedy, I tell the story of how Shattering the Glass™, my women's education company, came to be. What I didn't say was that Brilliant Technology Applied™ is her twin brother. Both companies were born on Memorial Day weekend 2008 in the Dreaming Room, led by Michael E. Gerber.

For those who have not heard of him, Michael Gerber is a business consultant and is best known as the author of *The E-Myth* and more recently, *Awakening the Entrepreneur Within*, which is the book the Dreaming Room workshop is based on. Bill and I had met

Michael a couple of months before and were invited to attend his transformational weekend event.

Our technology company at that time, Sirrus Consulting, was failing fast. Michael recommended we put it to sleep and we came up with a new venture called Brilliant Technology Applied (BTA™).

This transition started our transformation from everything we were doing wrong to doing the same things wrong but learning why they were wrong and more importantly what to do to change them and the outcome. Now we consciously and consistently apply these principles and are making better choices and are in control of our future. It has been a painful AND liberating process.

In the beginning, Bill and I were at each other's throats. Since we are two very strong personalities, both of us trying to lead the business made it look like a two-headed llama walking down the street sideways. It was horrible. Nothing got done and we were fighting fiercely with one another over control and direction of the company.

We hated our business. We hated our lives. We started to hate each other.

I even tried to leave the technology business. I concentrated on BTA's sister company, Shattering the Glass™, and I became a Women's Prosperity Network (WPN) chapter leader. Then I launched a series of women's business training seminars and last year I went out to San Diego and became a Michael Gerber certified facilitator for the Dreaming Room. I wanted anything but to be in the technology business.

The more I tried to leave, the more BTA™ pulled me back in. We landed large corporate clients and interesting projects. The demand was there for our products and our services. We were getting referrals from existing customers, and companies were looking to us for help.

But, in order for us to help them, Bill and I needed to be on the same page. BTA™ needed to be a team.

We needed to have a collective vision of where we wanted our company to go. We needed to assess exactly where we were then and chart a course to our desired destination. But most importantly, we needed to be able to communicate with each other.

This part was tough. Our relationship was teetering, yet we had to have this discussion. We had to get past this impasse and have a real conversation about our business. Our future depended on it. It couldn't wait any longer.

We finally sat down together and worked it out.

What we discovered during this process has become the key to moving our business forward. We want to share our results with you in hopes that you can use this discussion to shortcut your learning curve and be able to hit the ground running in your own company.

The biggest lesson Bill and I learned was that we have different personality styles and that we are dissimilar in the way we prefer information to be presented and received during our conversations. This realization was ground-breaking!

Then we realized this discovery could be applied to every area of our business, especially in sales.

That was when we came up with BTA4SALES™, our method of Brilliant Technology Applied™ for Sales.

S-A-L-E-S stands for:

S -Seduce

A - Ask

L - Listen

E - Explore the Possibilities

S - Solve their Problem

We would create a mental movie for the prospect by working with the seller to improve their "buying process". BTA™ would guide clients through their own customer's purchasing experience and help them fine tune it. Then BTA™ would put technology in place to support and automate the process. The result would be more sales and happier customers for our clients, and us.

By designing the sales process from the buyers' primary personality perspectives, we would be certain to meet their expectations. To do this we would need to get inside each buyer's head and walk a mile in her shoes.

SEDUCE

Seduction is the first step in the BTA4SALES™ process. You need to bring the buyers in like drawing bees to honey.

But how? What motivates a prospect to want to buy? What do they need to feel good about to make a purchase? And equally important, what stops them from saying "Yes"?

BTA™ discovered that what attracts prospects and makes them feel good about buying differs depending upon their personality style. What turns them off can be amplified by not receiving information in their preferred method of communication.

Determining the personality style of your prospect will help you craft the message and how you deliver it. You will also be able to match and mirror their buying expectations and achieve the desired result, which is a sale for you.

At the core of the BTA4SALES™ process is a behavior model similar to DISC (DISC is a quadrant behavioral model based on the work of Dr. William Moulton Marston (1893–1947). In the BTA-4SALES™ System, there are four basic personality types: Fire , Air , Water and Earth . Each style has particular preferences of why they buy, when they buy, whom they buy from, what they buy and how they want to interact.

People with the Fire behavior style are results oriented, risk takers, they like to win and be in control. They are fast paced and

173

F - FIRE

BTA™ Buyer Personality types.
Each table summarizes one of the Personality traits

Personality Traits	Results oriented, risk taker, likes to win, fast-paced, in control
Why they buy	See it and they want it, got to have it
When they buy	On the spot, preceived benefits
Who they buy from	Professionals, leaders in industry, punctual, prepared
What they buy	The best, most expensive, VIP package
Communication Preference	Bullets, charts, graphs, bottom line figures, return on investment
What turns them off	Babble, incompetence, no action, inauthenticity, lots of details
Drawn by	Prestige, luxury, mystique, one of a kind, value, power

A - AIR

Personality Traits	Loves to talk, likes attention, life of the party, social
Why they buy	New, cool, makes them look good
When they buy	Easy and affordable, when it feels good, entertained
Who they buy from	Optimistic, polite, fun, benefit social causes, name droppers
What they buy	Trends, shiny objects, love sales, shopaholics
Communication Preference	Phone calls, video, pictures, ask for their opinion, how do they feel
What turns them off	Details, lengthy sales process, boring people, paperwork
Drawn by	Recognition, stroking, lust and vice, incentives, shortcuts

W - WATER

Personality Traits	Patient, team player, low key, want harmony
Why they buy	Necessity, function, for others
When they buy	Slow, think it over, fear making a mistake, seek other opinions
Who they buy from	People they trust, do not rush, build relationships
What they buy	Gifts, bonuses and two-for-one sales so they can keep one
Communication Preference	Guarantees, testimonials, try before they buy, refunds, action plans
What turns them off	Pushy people, do not interrupt, hype
Drawn by	Reliability, reputation, ask to share feelings, positive impact on others

E - EARTH

Personality Traits	Task oriented, rules, details, like data
Why they buy	Quality, practical, make the right choice, logical
When they buy	After they research alternatives, comparisons, choices, documentation
Who they buy from	People with integrity, consistency, follow-up
What they buy	Efficient, long lasting, added value, save time
Communication Preference	Diagrams, statistics, reports, cost-benefit analysis
What turns them off	Goofy behavior, not serious, evasive answers
Drawn by	Specifics, roadmaps, processes, timetables

buy because they see it and have to have it. They buy the best and most expensive option and they usually buy on the spot. First impressions matter to them. Show them the bottom line and a quick return on investment (ROI). They like to see data in charts and graphs or bullets. Don't waste their time if you are not ready to write the order.

What can turn off an F is too much talk and not enough action. They are not interested in long, detailed reports, and if you are not professional in your appearance and delivery, they will discard you. They are drawn by mystique and prestige. They are turned off by inauthenticity and incompetence.

The A – Air style loves to talk, likes attention and is the life of the party. These buyers seek recognition and need to be stroked often. Do not bore them with details; instead show them shortcuts and trends. Make sure to thank them at every step. They buy what is new, cool or makes them look good as long as it is easy and affordable. They are shopaholics and love a sale, will attempt to rationalize their purchase. They will be attracted to items of lust and vice. Phone calls and DVDs work best for communicating with an Air personality type . Back your sale up with written correspondence, just in case. If there are too many steps in the buying process, they will bail.

Water – W types are patient and low-key. They make excellent team players and thrive on harmony. They buy due to necessity and function. Do not rush or interrupt them. They like to think things over, and are in fear of making a mistake. Trust is a big issue. Use testimonials and guarantees. They like to buy gifts for others. "Two for one" sales are excellent because often they will not purchase only for themselves.

The E – Earth personality likes to see data in diagrams and reports. The need to make sure they make the right choice and purchase only after doing extensive research and comparison shopping. They want items that improve efficiency, save time, are practical, last a long time and create added value. They want a choice, so offer them two solutions. No more than three or they will become confused and paralyzed. Do not act goofy, or they will not take you seriously.

This insight into personality type is so important because if you are primarily one personality style and your prospect is another you may not communicate easily since each of you requires something different from the conversation. Being aware of your own style and then identifying your buyer's style will put you in control of the sales process. You will learn to quickly adapt and give the buyer what they need to move forward toward a purchase.

Being aware of different personality types is also important in all of your communications, not just sales. It is especially useful when dealing with family members and co-workers.

For example, Bill is predominately an A – Air and I lean toward E – Earth, plus we both are solid F – Fire. If I started to talk about putting a plan together he would go into overwhelm mode. If he wanted to tell me a story about something, I would get bored half way through and ask him to just tell me the reader's digest version and then his feelings would get hurt.

No wonder we were having difficulty communicating and moving our business forward. We were both communicating the way we needed to receive information, not the way the *other* person needed to receive it. Now the two-headed llama walking down the street sideways makes sense.

So how can you apply this methodology to your business? Think about your main clients. What personality profile do they fall into? Are they more directing in nature (fire) or do they like to be on the team but not in the foreground (water)? Are they people oriented (air) or more focused on tasks (earth)? Knowing the answers to these questions, you can recognize what they need from you and make it easy for them to purchase your products and services.

The next four steps in the BTA4SALES™ process (A, L, E and S) are to engage the prospect in conversation and uncover their problem: to find out what ails, or "ALES" them. Buyers want solutions to their problems. They are in pain and need help. This includes asking questions, listening to the answers, exploring the possibilities and offering solutions.

In addition to uncovering the pain, it is necessary to reveal whether the buyer has the money and if the buyer has the power to make the purchasing decision.

For most salespeople, closing the sale is the stumbling block. Depending on your view of manners and money, this step can be very difficult. Many of us have difficulty selling because of our own hang-ups about money.

Converting a prospect into a customer can be the hardest part in the sales process. Fear sets in. We don't want to appear pushy or worse, desperate.

Getting answers to questions about pain, money and decision making now will save you time and effort down the road. If the buyer doesn't reveal themselves, you will spend a lot of time with someone who cannot buy from you.

Remember how you learned to tie your shoes? Selling is no different. This stage takes practice. But I promise if you use the BTA™ Buyer Personality tables, selling will become stress-free.

Let's look at each stage of the engagement process in more detail.

ASK

The second step in the BTA4SALES™ process is to Ask.

By asking the right questions at the right time you can guide your prospect through the buying maze. Picture a boat ride at Walt Disney's Magic Kingdom. Gates open and close to direct the boats in the correct direction as they go down the river. The speed of the water keeps the boat moving forward. You can place ramps, music, animated characters, waterfalls, detours and other items along the river ride to change direction and enhance the experience.

The same is true during the buying cycle. To illicit certain responses, you need to ask the right questions.

Use expanding questions when you need to gain more information. Ask questions like "How would you use this?" and "What does that mean to you?"

Use clarifying questions to confirm and summarize or to get agreement before continuing. Ask them to "Please give me an example of that?" or "I think I heard you say that . . ." or "Does that feel/look/sound good to you?"

If the conversation is going down the wrong path, use redirection questions to get back on track like "What if you could also do . . .?" or "What did I hear you mention before that?"

Reversing questions are also very powerful. They shift the focus, resolve objections and uncover the real issues by getting the buyer emotionally involved in the conversation. Questions like "Did I miss something?" or "How much would you anticipate something like this would cost?" or "What timeframe would be acceptable for a project of this caliber?"

The main objective of the Ask step is to discover the prospect's personality style. By the way he or she responds, you can then direct the conversation to discover their pain and how you can help them.

Use the personality style guidelines from the BTA™ Buyer Personality tables above when asking the prospective buyer questions. If you are not sure what personality style they are, start with an Earth question first, then move to a Fire question, then ask an Air question and finally a Water question. The prospect will respond enthusiastically to one or more of your questions.

Earth personalities will have a harder time with feeling and emotion questions but be quick on answering task or logical questions. Examples of Earth questions are "Which process are you most concerned with?" and "What is currently being done to address this problem?"

Fire personalities want you to get right to the point. The questions you ask Fire types should address the results the buyer wants to achieve like "What are your expectations of?" and "Where should we start?"

Air types want to chit-chat first and get to know you. You should ask questions like "Are you married or have kids?" or "What is your favorite sports team, movie, place to visit, etc.?" Once you satisfy their social need, you can ask more questions relevant to discovering their pain.

Water personalities are always thinking about the team. Water questions include other people like "Who else has the same problem?" and "What other benefits would be good for the group?"

Whatever questions you ask, the important part is how the buyer answers them.

LISTEN

Listening is the most important step in the BTA4SALES™ process. Communication from the seller should be 30% talk and 70% listen. There is more to learn by listening and observing than by talking.

Remember that whatever questions you ask your prospect the chances are they will lie at first. This is a self-protection mechanism and we all do it without thinking. You will have to be persistent to reveal the truth.

Earth and Water are the most reserved and tend to hide their feelings at first. They are much more comfortable talking about facts. An Earth type wants you to know they have everything under control and Water personalities are excited that you want to know more about them.

People with Air personalities may tend to give you the answer they think you wanted to hear. They are afraid you won't like them if they give you their opinion too quickly. Once they get to know you they will be telling you how everything should be.

Fire styles try to be nice at first and then let you have it. They can appear impatient and are just waiting for you to ask them a real question. Gain their respect by appearing confident. Be prepared to answer back with tough questions.

Remember that it takes two people to have a conversation. Know your own personality style and practice recognizing other people's styles through the way they answer your questions and ask their own.

Make a game out it. Try identifying friends, business associates and family members. Use the following summary and see which types you can identify. Then if they are willing, ask them to identify themselves and see how close you are.

Words that describe Fire types are competitive, demanding, impatient, determined, and independent. Air styles are emotional, friendly, compassionate, impulsive and talkative. A Water person is relaxed, dependable, diplomatic, loyal and at times shy. Earth personalities are intense, accurate, logical and thorough. They are perfectionists.

EXPLORE POSSIBILITIES

The fourth step in the BTA4SALES™ process is exploring the possibilities. The goal here is to develop trust. If buyers trust you, they will sell themselves. You can help them by eliminating the risk of doing business with you.

State how long you have been in the business and offer guarantees. Depending on the product or service you sell, have a pilot program or trial period. Use before and after comparisons, customer testimonials, current situation and projected future analysis, and have a frequently asked questions page.

Follow the BTA™ Buyer Personality types. Give the prospect what they need to move further along in the buying process. Eliminate the obstacles by knowing what the prospect needs out of the transaction.

SOLVE THEIR PROBLEM

The final stage of the BTA4SALES™ process is providing a collaborative solution. If all of the previous steps have been accomplished successfully, this becomes a no brainer.

When proposing your solution, you want to make sure the buyer's expectations have been met. This moment is important because you do not want buyer's remorse. Discovering the problem is critical to the success of the sale. Delivering your solution should assure the buyer they have made the right choice by going with you. Your product or service solves their problem.

With the BTA4SALES™ process you are creating a "Buyer Zone". Your prospects sell themselves and you reap the rewards.

This approach can be used in every area of your life. Especially when dealing with family members.

When Bill and I disagree, it is often because we are not paying attention to the other person's needs in the conversation. When we are open to the other person's personality style, we communicate on a very different level. This is why we find it so important to share our BTA4SALES program with you.

Bill and I live together, work together, shop together, play together, travel together, *OMG!* If we did not use the techniques I have described here we would have ended our relationship long ago. Instead, both our relationship and our business are growing. We are in better communication than ever before. Our BTA4SALES™ process is working. It can work for you too.

Remember, selling is about meeting the expectations of your buyers by delivering the message in the format that they need. Understanding what motivates prospects to make a purchase and what turns them off gives you the freedom to structure the conversation around what is comfortable for them. Communicating with buyers the way they want to be communicated with will take the focus off of you and make it easier for you to share your products and services.

BECCA TEBON (aka: F.I.T.preneur)

As a Wellness Lifestyle Coach and Fitness Trainer, Becca Tebon has been coined the F.I.T.preneur, and it is her mission to help people shift their lifestyles to a greener, healthier more Selfull existence, from the inside out, by sharing hands-on usable, techniques, trainings, questionnaires, and ceremonies.

She helps you combat:

5) Asthma	7) Chronic fatigue	9) Weight Issues
6) Eczema/psoriasis	8) Type II Diabetes	10 Heart Health... and so many other diseases.

Learn how to turn your body into the strong temple it was created to be, and how you can how you can avoid cancer and other diseases by simply changing your body's pH WITH FOOD.

As a veteran brand developer and owner of a successful national advertising agency, Becca is available to speak publically for organizations and businesses interested in learning and showing how better self care creates a healthy lifestyle with more focus, clarity, optimizing results, energy as well as the good ole "Happiness Meter." It is her intention and mission to create and support you with products and services that offer hands-on, simple baby steps that will manifest and help you live a healthier and happier life.

You can learn more about her philosophy, "The Five Pillars of Wellness: Mind, Body, Energy, Nutrition and Green Living" and programs on her website where she shares her personal triumphs over multiple congenital health issues to pave the way for others to also gain control through prevention and natural remedies.

She has served on many national organizations promoting safer, healthier and better ways to support people and the planet

- WE Campaign
- HEALTHY CHILD/HEALTHY WORLD Program
- National Asthma Coalition
- Wyland Foundation

All programs have a 100% Money-back guarantee and deliver simplicity and results!

Education/Certifications:

- University of Florida - Journalism/Advertising
- AFAA - Aerobic and Fitness Association of America -Certified Group Fitness/Trainer Certification

- ACE - American Council on Exercise -Personal Trainer Certification
- Lemond - Group Cycling Instructor Certification
- Power Pilates - Fitness Instructor Certification
- AFPA - American Fitness Professionals & Associates - Group Aqua Certification

Her extraordinary friendly demeanor creates a unique experience for all that are seeking to find a simpler, healthier and greener lifestyle.

Phone: 561-289-8822

Email: Becca@BeccaTebon.com

Facebook: http://preview.tinyurl.com/7kq2e4f

Twitter: http://twitter.com/BeccaTebon

Linked in: http://www.linkedin.com/in/fitpreneur

YouTube: http://www.youtube.com/user/beccateboninc

Be Well. F.I.T. And Green from the Inside Out!

DEDICATION

I am a reflection of and thankful to my three daughters, family and friends who support me on my journey and share my dreams. I dedicate this to my grandfather, Sam Simon , my grandmother, Elaine Simon, and my dad, who all mentored me in various ways throughout their lives, and through their transition to a higher place, I clearly saw my purpose here on Earth.

Your vision are
golden & purposeful!
Stay on your mission.

Chapter Eleven

Let's Take a Trip and Lose Your Baggage

by Becca Tebon

This just in.... Or in my case might be better written, THIS JUST OUT! Just like you, my life has had LOTS of experiential moments, highs and MANY swurvy, curvies (unmarked turns), that have brought me to the place Iam now. "Iam" refers to the biblical sense of being that we honor that of what we were created for and live in intention to use our unique purpose and passions to support others. I wrote this chapter with the hope that through reading it, you begin to discover YOUR "Iam" and realize that the journey of life can be brilliantly landscaped, full of learning and growing. Turn on your positive meter and truly ENjoy the ride!

I am often heard saying "Lose Your Baggage From the Inside Out," because that is precisely what I have done for myself and others, and hope to shed (pun intended) some light on this subject for you. Losing the extra pounds on the outside FOREVER BATTLE will only occur when thought and behavior shift! In this chapter, I will teach you how to MIND MAP, a POWerful tool that will help you visualize and seek clarity for your goals, as well as develop the baby-steps necessary to place them into ACTION and garner the results you are seeking.

Hi, I am Becca Tebon and am excited to share some of the proven tools, tested techniques and simple baby steps from my book, *From the Pillow to the Podium*. But first let me share some of my titles, past and present, not limited to, and in no particular order:

- CIA: Chief Inspirational Officer to three amazing souls who I call my children
- CEO: Owned a highly successful national advertising / marketing agency for 12 years
- Wife (now happily single)
- Certified Personal Trainer and Group Fitness Instructor for 27 years
- Green Goddess all my life
- Green Soccer Mom thanks to my all-star athlete, Chloe
- Speaker
- Natural Health Advocate
- Entrepreneur
- Fitness Model/Athlete
- God's Girl, Daughter and Friend

What's in a title? I have never been one to understand why someone's TRUE importance was based on what their title states. Don't you agree we need to appreciate someone based on their value system and actions towards others? So why did I start my chapter with this seemingly insignificant statement? It's simple - it is VERY

IMPORTANT!! "WE" are placed into a "box" by people we come in contact with based on titles and appearances. Isn't it sadly true, our opinion of ourselves can be swayed, based on the thoughts and beliefs which are held by others about us!!!! (Read that 4X more times) Want to lose your baggage and gain your **IAM**? Let's go!

LET'S GET REAL: MAPPING THE UNMARKED CURVES

From a very young age we are coined with accolade and failure statements such as,

"You are such a good (fill in the blank)!"

"Why can't you finish the simple (fill in the blank), but your brother can (fill in the blank)?"

"Why didn't you try harder?"

Can you relate to any of these? Ever say them to your children or others? That might be a sore spot. Okay, I will open up MANY sore spots. Getting real, opening up and being vulnerable is NOT easy, but I can promise you one thing — YOU WILL COME OUT THE WINNER! Seeing you in a new lighter, brighter and happier place, available to create REALationships and develop a healthy flow and glow from within! Are you ready?

Friends, life hasn't always rolled so well for me; in fact chaos could have been my middle name. Nothing came easy to me; however, I never gave up! If I wanted something, I figured out the most lucrative way to obtain it, and lucrative means blood, sweat and tears! I created the vision (I will teach you this later on) and I kept focused. Always asking, learning and putting into practice what I wanted in my life that I learned to attract. I hope by sharing my authentic, vulnerable self, it will allow you to GET REAL TO THE CORE with your gorgeous self! Sit down and grab a cup of coffee or perhaps a green microbiotic drink, we got some catching up to do!

The elementary years were tough. I missed nearly 30% of school because I was born sickly. I was plagued with Chronic Asthmatic

Bronchitis, skeletal problems, which caused pains all over my body down to my feet, and digestive problems that had me keeled over in pain. I was diagnosed with a form of dyslexia and had speech problems, which got me pulled out of class through third grade.

In fourth grade I took control of my own rah-rahing and joined softball, sports it seemed was my area to thrive, since my older brother took the "brainiac" position. Now I gotta tell you, I had never played, and I wasn't very good, but a friend convinced me to try out for her team. Little did she know that sports would become a major influence on how I found myself later in life and a MAJOR catalyst into my purpose for feeling good about myself AND helping others! (Thank you, Lisa DiLorenzo!)

I was actually so terrible at bat, the coach had me bunt (I think my teammates were hoping I'd get hit with a loose pitch, because it assured them I'd get on base). I was gifted with rather quick legs, perfect for stealing bases, so I was adorned with the nickname "Giselle." I was decent in the outfield and had quite an arm, my saving grace, so I wasn't completely embarrassed.

All-in-all the good feelings I had were still overpowered by negative self-conscious thoughts. Do you feel like that now? My teeth were crooked and my lower jaw protruded, my skin was full of blemishes, and I had three major growth spurts. I was tall, lanky, awkward, pimply, and sickly and felt VERY insecure. I was not the confident, Godly woman Iam today. Nor did I feel important. Or smart. Do you carry insecure, inefficient, ineffective thoughts in your suitcase? Is this your internal picture now?

When I played softball and later championed track and field, I forgot about all of those voices. I forgot about all the things I couldn't do well, and I practiced for hours to perfect my throws, ground ball techniques and batting. Sports was (and still is) a place I could make declarations and stick to my vision, to drive my passions and quest for better... to excel. I didn't call them "declarations" then, however, that is exactly what they were.

I became a jockette, a natural choice! I was known for my sport abilities, often picked before my older brother by the guys on the block to play football, kickball or any sport (yea) and always the team captain or "selected" to play on a team. A highlight was being invited to try out for the All-Star team my second year. I did make the team, but sat the bench, unless they needed someone to steal bases. I was thrilled to be on the team and cheer my friends on!! I MADE IT!!! With more practice the next year, I pitched and batted seventh. By the fourth year, I played pitcher, third base, first base or left outfield, made the All-star team and batted 6th. Does it sound like I had determination, dedication, and drive to be the best I could be? It took me four years to get a starting position on the All-Star team... but I got there and am still proud and remember it like it was yesterday. What will it take to get you to garner something you really want or need to do but have not gone for it for one reason or another?

That SAME FEELING is in my soul today when I declare ANY-THING I wish to achieve. It is a buzz like no other. It is INSIDE ME and it is inside you too. For example, let's take running. Most of us can walk, some can run. However, if you aren't taught the simplest way to run, wear the attire and given simple attainable instructions and goals you won't like running or give up because it hurts or isn't easy. If you can walk I will get you running whether physically on the pavement, in a pool or mentally in your mind by strengthening your Mind Muscle! I was eager to achieve, to have fun (always a priority) and was always very coachable. My pure passion and ability to sit back and take direction from mentors and coaches has served me well all my life. *People want to help people who want to be helped.* READ THAT SENTENCE FOUR MORE TIMES, then proceed!!! People will only change when they are surrounded with like-minded supportive people so decide you are coachable and ready to learn and seek out people who you resonate with!

Even a coach needs a coach. We are all students and teachers. Don't dismiss that which you don't know, like or understand for it may be inside THAT area you will find your greatest power.

In this chapter we will begin the process of finding your Selfullness™ that will determine your passions and purpose. You will see how you can PROFIT from selfullness. Profit is the gold within that delivers you peace of mind, body, energy, health and living! Stay focused, grab a pencil, because we are gonna work today!

Yup, I might have been born with my glass 3/4 full, but I realized mine was that full just in case some spilled out along those rugged, swurvy curvy paths I would take! I wasn't the neatest kid on the block.... LOTS spilled out, especially over the past few years; but I share tools to replenish the glass in my first book, *From the Pillow to the Podium*. Seek to find the goodness and light in every situation. Close friends often call me because they know I will be able to paint a picture that brings a smile and sense of security and clarity. My first message is, DON'T HAVE THIN SKIN! I had the thinnest skin, was often hurt, humiliated and left without a voice. Even today, I find my voice is quieted under certain situations or people, but guess what? I have tools in my workout bag that turn that around every time. It's comforting knowing I now have a "go to place" that brings me a smile inside AND brings me back to the place I can evolve. Having spent 15 years in an unhappy marriage, second guessing myself, feeling put down and left alone, and where my dreams didn't feel important or even sought out, I felt my drive tucked inside and in a state of turmoil. It was his needs to take care of the family, gain respect amongst others, and make a good living that pushed my needs to the side. I allowed it. My ex-husband is a great person but didn't understand how to get what he needed from me nor did I ever feel authentic sharing myself with him. This soaring butterfly was in a cocoon. I feared showing my needs and felt rejected more and more. I shifted my reliance to another person, which is something one should never do. Happiness is something WE create for ourselves, with the support of others, but not reliant on another. I also found that to truly be glorified to help others, I needed to go through a few more transformations. I like to refer to them as *UNMARKED CURVES* on our road to the great Iam. Yes, this caterpillar did transform into a butterfly, and you will too; however, Iam here to assure you that my true transformation was within the past two years (and continues), and your awakening, enlightenment and transitions will be an ongoing process as well! Longtime friends say I look different and that I radiate after going through my swurvy curvy, mind bending incidents which started October 2009 and finished the year off truly with a bang on 12/31/09. Gotta admit, these experiences weren't by choice, however, Iam truly blessed that they did happen. Swimming in my full glass of water helped me to see the goodness that was to shine through. God, or whoever you choose to call upon as a higher being of faith and support, was the one that kept the water glass full and showered me with love, forgiveness, a beautiful heart, and ironically, showed me that ALL of my experiential moments, unmarked turns, health issues and learned skills would be the very things I needed to be the Wellness Lifestyle Coach Iam so grateful and excited to be today.

I WAS BORN INTO WELLNESS

Yes, I've been in fitness and wellness since age seven; however, I was on the other side of the coin loaded with medications, steroids, needles and always (or so it felt) at doctors' offices since birth. It was NORMAL for me to have some kind of something put on a teaspoon EVERYDAY!!! Now, proudly, 40 years later Iam completely off all medications for my asthmatic bronchitis for the past six years.

I found by removing triggers and using natural remedies I have "cured" myself and hundreds of others, including my two youngest also put on steroids as infants for breathing complications! My chronic life-long skeletal pain took a bit longer; however, today Iam pain-free and took up running after a 12-year sabbatical. My body is loaded with arthritis, bursitis, scoliosis, stenosis, degenerative bones and slipped disks in my neck. I had a complete meniscus removal, yet Iam pain free and thriving ... even Running! I coach others how to train effectively and safely avoiding injuries, strengthening their temples, losing weight, sculpting and building endurance. I speak on how to get a greener life by getting rid of toxins that trigger and contribute to all of the above! Remember, the value of being green is self-preservation, for you and Mother Earth!

So that's how I became a Wellness Lifestyle Coach; I was granted it from birth and have helped hundreds. It is my mission to help thousands upon thousands. Would you like to acquire some tools that will help you discover your HAPPY, HEALTHY SELF - your SELFULLNESS™?

It's time to get your inner voice back, get on track and understand how to THRIVE in this life not just survive day to day! Get ready, we are gonna fill your glass up and discover the passions and purpose for which you were created! I was blessed with and have found through the years it is something that can be taught, granted to others and skillfully honed by anyone who is ready to be coached.

IAM A LIFESTYLE TRANSFORMER

You've just read my story. What does yours sound like? We all have experiences, the only difference is HOW we process them and what WE DO to move forward, and CREATE the lives we were purposed for and want to live!!! That is precisely why I developed and share my *90-day F.I.T.system Proven, Proprietary and 100% Money Back Guaranteed Weight Loss and Lifestyle Wellness Program.* No matter what your strengths or soft spots might be, I promise you that all thoughts and living things are created by energy, vibration and transmitted by the brain and heart. How you learn to use your energy and thoughts will be the #1 factor to what will transpire in your life both externally and internally. Energy is the core. Are you ready to build your **Mind-Muscle**™ portion of your SELFULLESS?

Our mind is so powerful but like other muscles in our body, if left untrained, will not bring us optimum potential. The constant I have seen and now address, is the need to organize the thought process so it runs smoother, in sync and less reactive, and is more responsive as people fuel their bodies with good nutrition AND good thoughts AND actions!! Learning to be RESPONSIVE allows much greater pleasure and freedom in all arenas. Soar with me on a course that will place you on the path you want, through baby steps. In a world full of quick remedies, instant gratification, seamless unsatisfying conveniences, we need to unlock your suitcase and throw out the garbage! Your BIG picture is magnificent so take 90 days to build it and get it ready for presenting to the world! 100% guaranteed — I stake my name, reputation and your outcome on the 90 Day Wellness and Weight Loss Transformation! If I could promise you change, would you want it? Would you invest 90 days to get it?

I spent over a year developing, tweaking and testing my unique, interactive system that I guarantee works to help those going through transitions and steer through those unseen swurvy curves in life. Each system delivers results as unique as the individual who is engaged in it!! Let's face it; we own different stories, experiences, and events that attach meaning to our daily walk. The most important thing isn't what you've done; it's what you want to do? Where do you want to go? Give? Receive?

Yea, you've reached the place where I will now help you discover your SELFULLNESS™! This is my gift to you and I hope it will reveal some simple ways to position yourself, gain posture, clarification, enlightenment and POWer to you! It contains some of the proprietary elements within the F.I.T.mind Program. It is my sincere hope and intention for you to have an "aha moment." To realize something POWerful within you, a new way to gain insight and know what "happy" looks like and FEELS like! I believe that transformation, true expansive transitions take place through interactive, hands-on tools. So grab a cool beverage, note pad and pencil, we have some get real, expressive, expository developments about to take place. Put your cape on because you are about to SOAR!

COMMIT TO YOUR SELFULLNESS™

Selfullness. This is the single most powerful investment we can ever make in life, an investment in ourselves! It is the only instrument we have within us, that costs NOTHING and can transform EVERYTHING!!

SELF-CARE ISN'T SELFISH! Selfullness is about putting yourself first. Does that sound selfish? If you were raised to put others before yourself, then you might have a hard time with this concept. Please keep reading!!! I PROMISE, by the end of this paragraph it will all make sense. Fair enough? Good! Because I want you to know YOU COUNT! Look, Iam one of the least selfish people I know (really, MANY gut checks later I can honestly say this). Many moons ago, I was in a very single state of mind and clearly decided everything based on my own end result which is MUCH different than being selfull! Today, Iam the world's best friend, helper, inspirer, and encourager. I will stop everything to get a friend out of a mess, lend an ear, drive their kid to a soccer tournament, or cook a meal for an ill neighbor. You get the message. Iam selfull!

All your thoughts, needs, beliefs and actions need to be fueled with the right passion. It is not possible to keep going and going like the energizer bunny without stopping at the give me energy depot from time to time to evaluate what's going on and contemplate how the next stage will look and feel. For most of us, however, the idea of taking time to replenish our energy and direction seems like a luxury we can't afford, or haven't prioritized its importance in the context of all the others things on our to do list. In truth, it is only when we take notice of our needs for selfullness and make it a non-negotiable priority that we can put forth the very best of ourselves, our passions and discover our purpose. Everyone in your proximity will benefit when you acquire SELFULLNESS! The quality of our relationships and our level of efficiency, clarity, and productivity are magnified when we approach life from a sense of the cup runneth over versus the meter is about to expire.

THE IMPORTANCE OF THE WORD DELETE

DE•LETE /di'lēt/

Synonyms:

erase - cancel - obliterate - efface - expunge

Verb:

Remove or obliterate (text), esp. by drawing a line through it

The acronym for D.E.L.E.T.E. is anything but negative. Deleting is the positive, empowering action one takes on creating boundaries, prioritizing oneself and supporting one's most basic needs, that will enhance one's SELFULLNESS™.—Becca Tebon

Do It... This is your life, take responsibility!

Expand ... to your greatness. Discover and use your gifts!

Love ... Always come from the heart (not from anger, judgment or the past)

Energy ... Realize that everything needs and depends on ENERGY. Learn how to create and attract the positive sources!

Think ... Envision and dream that which you desire. Learn how to use your mind to create Manifestations!

Extraordinary ... Be the authentic you, transcend into the greatness of your Selfullness!

199

I created the "Great Iam" and want to share it with you because I have seen the shift not only in myself, but in countless others with whom I have shared this philosophical movement. We need to pay attention to how much positive energy we are taking in and assess how much energy output is required of us. When we focus on what we want to achieve, we provide authentic direction and support to those in our journey. Evaluating your energy management and understanding the need to fuel this before trying to provide for others on an empty, or seemingly empty, passionless way without getting in touch with yourself, your needs, desires and driven purpose will cause you to feel empty, lost or worthless.

First, I need you to know you are blessed. YOU were created for a purpose. You are special. And that you are needed... And needed to be full of you!!! When did someone last give you permission to be full of yourself? And how do those words make you feel — right now? Stop and think about it. If you don't think you are 100%, don't act with verve, passion and directed precision 100% of the time, and aren't concerned with being 100% then who loses? What true value will you be? What value will be perceived by others and where will it get you at the end of the day? In addition, you need to pay attention to unnecessary sources of energy loss, like people, places and things that deplete your spirit and cause negative self-talk, thoughts or actions. So climb aboard! You are going on a journey about YOU!!!! You are the next million dollar person. Let's go!

COMMIT TO YOU!

"Being SELFULL is a navigable priority in which I will focus on daily by setting INTENTions and being present!" — Becca Tebon

Write this on a note card and place on your mirror, adding YOUR NAME in place of mine.

Selfullness is *mastering* our emotional, physical, thought-provoking, spiritual and environmental energies; it is caring for, nurturing, loving, and showing affection to us in order to support and fill our main tank to its optimal level. So let's agree being *SELFULL is a navigable priority in which we will focus.* You are promising yourself to push through the questions in this chapter... And NOT SKIP ANY!! Deal?

Commit NOW to striving forward with baby steps and setting aside time to do the exercises that are physical, emotional, mental, environmental and energetically uplifting to reshape your lifestyle. You are moving forward and everyone in your journey will see the shift and reap the benefits too! Unless you do so, your health, productivity, REALationships, and mental and emotional well-being will undoubtedly suffer.

I like to give people one last day to "be" the way they are. Take inventory of how you feel. Enjoy your day. Cry it out. Today is the last day that you will be like this, feel this way, internalize this way. You will no longer move through the ROUTINE OF THE DAY like it doesn't carry importance or meaning... Like YOU don't carry importance of meaning!!! Tomorrow is amazing! And EVERY tomorrow after that will be too. Sign below and get ready to soar!!!

_____

Your Special Signature   Date of Your Declaration

List WHY you want to make changes: (i.e.: I want to make changes because I feel like I am letting my life get away from me; I don't like the way I look or feel.) _____

_____

_____

_____

_____

_____ .

LIST the TOP FIVE things you will change: (list as many as you want... Just focus on FIVE to start with)

1._____

2._____

3._____

4._____

5._____

The REWARD you get when you are done with this chapter: (and taking actions to incorporate the change of your top FIVE WHY's)

_____

_____

_____

_____

_____

_____.

READY? SET? ACTION!

1. **DECLARE IT!** *Declare* this week as your time to begin focusing on your SELFULLNESS.

2. **ANALYZE!** Look at what is draining you. Choose one from the following list or come up with your own. Focus on it for one full week.

- Say "Yes!" when you mean "no."
- One-sided relationships
- Put off doing an old hobby
- Eating Junk food
- Watch too much television
- People pleasing
- Clutter
- Negative self-talk
- Spend more money than you make

- Not sleeping enough
- Over schedule
- Gossip
- Resentments
- Unfinished Paperwork

3. **ANALYZE SOME MORE!!** Look at what pumps you, what feels good and makes you smile. Choose one from the following list or come up with your own, and make the decision to ADD these into your energy reserves by doing this activity as often as possible this week.

- Slow down
- Breathe deeply
- Give up caffeine
- Prioritize
- Exercise
- Listen to music
- Drink water
- Eat HEALTHY for your temple
- Get a full night's rest
- Meditate/Yoga
- Read a good novel
- Learn a new skill, hobby, sport
- Journal
- Take a warm bath
- Practice mindfulness (being present)

4. **SET INTENTIONS!** Make renewing the physical, mental, nutrition, energy and environment a supreme, non-negotiable priority, ideal, thought and activity in your life daily! *Wake up 5 minutes early and MAKE the time to see your day and how you will use it and*

how you will feel!!! **This is #1 on my To-Do List every day!** WRITE YOUR INTENTIONS IN A JOURNAL and keep next to your bed.

By putting your Selfullness at the top of your list, you will build the energy reserves necessary for you to succeed in your relationships, business and personal life.

12 TIPS TO TRANSFORM YOUR THINK TANK

1. Mistakes are more than OKAY!

Mistakes teach you important lessons. The biggest mistake you can make is doing nothing because you're too scared. In life, it's rarely about getting a chance; it's about taking a chance. You'll never be 100% sure it will work, but you can always be 100% sure doing nothing will leave you standing in the same place at the same pace forever!

2. Discover your passion and your purpose and you will never have to work again!

As I offer my children some real career advice, I tell them not to base their career choice on other people's ideas, goals and recommendations. The right career choice is based on one key point: Finding hard work you love doing. As long as you remain true to yourself, and follow your own interests and values, you can find success through your passionate purpose.

3. Invest in your Selfullness™!

You are simply the product of what you know. The more time, energy and money you spend acquiring pertinent knowledge, the more control you have over your life.

4. Explore! Expand! Expose!

Your natural human fears of failure and embarrassment will sometimes stop you from trying new things. Rise above these fears, for your life's story is simply the culmination of many small, unique, swurvy curvy experiential moments. Not doing so is not living!

5. *People are not mind readers.*

People will never know how you feel, what you need or want them to do unless you tell them. Period. It really is that simple.

6. *Make declarations and take immediate action!*

Either you're going to take action and seize new opportunities, or someone else will. There's a huge difference between knowing how to do something and actually doing it. Knowledge is basically useless without action! (I know this one far too well!)

7. *Change is a constant!*

That's the one thing you can count on. However good or bad a situation is now, it will change. How you respond makes ALL the difference of how you will experience it! So look for and EMBRACE change. Seek the good in EVERY swurvy curve!

8. *Don't worry too much about what other people think about you.* What is important is how you feel about you. When we consider what others think, it clouds your energy and being. There is ONLY one YOU. Be authentic. Stay positive and go to your gratitude and selfull list of things as often as necessary!

9. *Be honest with yourself... Authenticity rocks!*

Living in a plastic world creates ambiguity (hmmm, know this one too). Get real, show emotions, be vulnerable and discover your purpose! These all lead to *priceless* peace of mind!

10. *Meditate!*

Sit, run, or lie alone in silence for at least five to ten minutes every day. Use this time to think, plan, reflect, and dream. With quiet, you can hear your thoughts, you can reach deep within yourself, and you can focus on mapping out the next logical, productive step in your life or find a much needed solution.

11. *Respect others and make them feel good.*

Supporting, guiding, and making contributions to other people is one of life's greatest rewards. Treat everyone with the same level of respect you give to a mentor or grandfather.

12. Be who you were born to be.

I left the most important one for last!!! You must follow your heart, and be who you were born to be. Listen to your intuition. You were born with talents, skills and GIFTS. To truly be happy, it is your destiny to discover, nurture, and hone in on YOUR GIFT and utilize it in a capacity that brings you true happiness, peace of mind and supports others. We were born with a purpose and many gifts that accentuate this purpose.

MAP OUT YOUR "I AM" (Please grab your notebook)

1.   List the gifts you were given. Start each sentence with "Iam great at_____. I bet you can list 10, 20... 50+ things!!!

2.   Things you started, wanted to start, or didn't start because someone or something made it seem impossible. (List at least 10)

3.   Make a LIFE LIST!!! Go ahead, all the things you've always wanted to do, places you want to travel to, things you'd like to see, touch or smell. Include things to champion your fears. I was afraid of drowning, so I got certified to scuba dive. Iam fearful of heights, I will not allow it to prohibit me from skiing and I will zip line in Costa Rica one day soon! I want to drive a race car, go to a shooting range, and learn how to play golf... Make YOUR LIFE LIST! I suggest Googling "fun things to do" or "fun place to go." You might even want to see what someone else put on their list (it isn't cheating, it's exciting)!

CREATING YOUR F.I.T.MIND MAP

Mapping out your thoughts, you create a visual that allows you to see and experience your mind more vividly, thus showing you — YOU CAN DO IT! Set aside 30 minutes, find a comfortable place that elicits your creativeness.

MATERIAL NEEDED:
- Unlined paper; 11 x 17 or larger
- Medium felt-tip markers or pens in a variety of colors
- Crayons, colored pencils, clippings from magazines or stuff/words collected that represents the topic

Step 1: Starting at the core of the theme, place a shape, illustration of word that represents your topic in the CENTER of the PAPER. For this example, Place YOUR NAME in the center.

Step 2: Next choose items from #2 or #3 above as links to you. For each one you write place, a shape, illustration of word that represents your topic, color it, or paste something that elicits it next to the word.

Step 3: Continue doing this for each. Sometimes words or themes will have connections, so connect them with a bridged line of color. Delve into how it will look, feel and even when you want to do it.

I hope you did the exercises I shared in this chapter. To move forward, it is vital to create a plan. Creating your map will give you the plan to discover and uncover many things that will bring happiness to your journey! Remember to laugh when you can, apologize when needed, and let go of what you can't change. Life is unpredictable, full of swurvy curvies, and lots of lessons to enrich us. Yet, it passes by in a flash, is full of grace, beauty and amazing creations and people. Set intentions at the start of each and every day (5-10 minutes) for what you want to see, feel, experience in that day. Make time to expand yourself, never get stagnant. Keep learning. Don't depend on another to create your happiness. Share your blessings with others, and be open to allow others to share theirs with you. Never stop being the student. Enlightenment is the glow within. Finally, don't let the past hinder your tomorrow. Forgiveness does not change the past, but it will enlarge and expand your future.

Today you are moving on from something! Learn to live in the present and you will learn how to be happy! Always refuel your tank and enjoy the ride. Utilize YOUR Great Iam. Namaste, Becca

Grab your free "WHAT ARE MY GIFTS" assessment by sending me an email at *FITpreneur@BeccaTebon.com* and write "FREE GIFT ASSESSMENT - AYSTS" in the subject line. I personally found it to be so enlightening and POWerful, so I want to share it with you!

CONCLUSION

Kimberly West is known as the "Soul See-er" & "Momma Butterfly" by many. She is passionate about co-creating a sacred space, that teaches YOU how to ALLOW Your Spirit and Vision to Soar!

www.AllowYourSpiritToSoar.com

At the release of this book in 2012, we are experiencing a *HUGE Global Shift*. A large percentage of people have lost their jobs, homes and even their lives. Many are struggling to recreate themselves by coming out of the darkness to be awakened to the light. My intentions of this book it to empower those who are struggling and help embrace the possibilities by trusting "the Voice" INside of YOU! As you have read these chapters, I pray you have been given a myriad of different perspectives and tips, tools and techniques you can incorporate into your lives so you can finally ALLOW Your Spirit & Vision to Soar! Welcome home my friends, welcome home.

With my entire Spirit and Soul, WE love you so!
Kimberly West aka Momma Butterfly